First World War
and Army of Occupation
War Diary
France, Belgium and Germany

41 DIVISION
Divisional Troops
190 Brigade Royal Field Artillery
5 May 1916 - 29 October 1919

WO95/2625/4

The Naval & Military Press Ltd
www.nmarchive.com
Published in association with The National Archives

Published by

The Naval & Military Press Ltd

Unit 10 Ridgewood Industrial Park,

Uckfield, East Sussex,

TN22 5QE England

Tel: +44 (0) 1825 749494

www.naval-military-press.com

www.nmarchive.com

This diary has been reprinted in facsimile from the original. Any imperfections are inevitably reproduced and the quality may fall short of modern type and cartographic standards.

© Crown Copyright
Images reproduced by permission of The National Archives, London, England, 2015.

Contents

Document type	Place/Title	Date From	Date To
Heading	41st Division 190th Brigade R.F.A. May 1916-Oct 1917 Mar 1918-1919 Oct Italy 1917 Nov-1918 Feb		
Heading	WO95/2625/5 41 Div 190 Bde RFA May 1916-Oct 1917		
War Diary	Havre	05/05/1916	06/05/1916
War Diary	Dradelles	07/05/1916	27/05/1916
War Diary	In The Field	16/06/1916	30/06/1916
War Diary		01/06/1916	30/06/1916
War Diary	In The Field	01/07/1916	31/08/1916
War Diary	L'Etoile	01/09/1916	01/09/1916
War Diary	Longpre	02/09/1916	02/09/1916
War Diary	Dernancourt	03/09/1916	06/09/1916
War Diary	Bazentin Le Grand	07/09/1916	15/09/1916
War Diary	Near Longueval	16/09/1916	30/09/1916
War Diary	Longueval	01/10/1916	06/10/1916
War Diary	Near Flers	07/10/1916	31/10/1916
War Diary	Longueval	01/11/1916	01/11/1916
War Diary	Bonnay	02/11/1916	03/11/1916
War Diary	Moulliens	04/11/1916	04/11/1916
War Diary	Ampliers	05/11/1916	05/11/1916
War Diary	Ligny-Sur Canche	06/11/1916	06/11/1916
War Diary	Fontaine	06/11/1916	06/11/1916
War Diary	Fontaine Lez Boulans	07/11/1916	09/11/1916
War Diary	Guardbecque	09/11/1916	10/11/1916
War Diary	Staples	10/11/1916	11/11/1916
War Diary	Boeschepe	11/11/1916	13/11/1916
War Diary	Near Dickebusch	14/11/1916	31/12/1916
War Diary	Dickebusch	01/01/1917	09/01/1917
War Diary	La Clytte	10/01/1917	23/01/1917
War Diary	Ryveld	24/01/1917	13/02/1917
War Diary	La Clytte	14/02/1917	28/02/1917
Miscellaneous	Report Of Raid On The Hollandscheshurr Redoubt	24/02/1917	24/02/1917
War Diary	La Clytte	01/03/1917	23/03/1917
War Diary	Sheet 28 N1a 3.2.	24/03/1917	08/04/1917
War Diary	N1a 32	09/04/1917	13/04/1917
War Diary	Muncq-Nieurlet South of Audruicq	14/04/1917	20/04/1917
War Diary	Muncq Nievlet	21/04/1917	23/04/1917
War Diary	Oehtezeele	24/01/1917	24/01/1917
War Diary	Sheet 28 N1a 3.2.	25/04/1917	06/05/1917
War Diary	S.E L O L H.2. H28d 7.8	06/05/1917	07/05/1917
War Diary	S. Eloi Group Headquarters	08/05/1917	10/05/1917
War Diary	St. Eloi Group H.2.	11/05/1917	12/05/1917
War Diary	St Eloi Group Headquarters.	12/05/1917	14/05/1917
War Diary	St. Eloi Group H.2.	14/05/1917	17/05/1917
War Diary	Seloi Headquarters	17/05/1917	19/05/1917
War Diary	St Eloi H.2.	19/05/1917	28/05/1917
War Diary	Southern Camp. Seloi	29/05/1917	31/05/1917
War Diary	A Group HQ. 41st D.A. H28.d.7.8	01/06/1917	02/06/1917
War Diary	A Group HQ.	03/06/1917	10/06/1917
War Diary	O.1a 6.4	11/06/1917	18/06/1917

War Diary	I 31 C 45.30	19/06/1917	25/06/1917
War Diary	H 36 C 31	26/06/1917	30/06/1917
War Diary	I 31 C 45.30	01/07/1917	20/07/1917
War Diary	O1b 6.9E	21/07/1917	28/07/1917
War Diary	O1b 60.95	29/07/1917	31/07/1917
Miscellaneous	To Headquarters, 41st Divisional Artillery.	02/09/1917	02/09/1917
War Diary	O.1b. 60.95	01/08/1917	31/08/1917
Miscellaneous	To Headquarters 41st Division.	02/12/1917	02/12/1917
War Diary	West Becourt	01/09/1917	13/09/1917
War Diary	H 33d 8.3	13/09/1917	13/09/1917
War Diary	I 29c. 6.4	14/09/1917	19/09/1917
War Diary	I 29c 6.4	14/09/1917	23/09/1917
War Diary	I 29C 6.4 H 33d 8.3	24/09/1917	30/09/1917
War Diary	H 33d 8.3. I 23a 60.65	01/10/1917	14/10/1917
War Diary	Coxyde Balins	15/10/1917	17/10/1917
War Diary	(Sheet 11 S.E.) R 29b 7.4	18/10/1917	20/10/1917
War Diary	R.29b 7.4	28/10/1917	31/10/1917
Miscellaneous	To Headquarters, 41st Divisional Artillery.	31/10/1917	31/10/1917
Heading	WO95/2625/6 41 Div 190 Bde RFA March 1918-Oct 1919		
Heading	41st Div. Bde. returned with Div. from Italy 8/12.3.18. War Diary Headquarters, 190th Brigade, R.F.A. March 1918		
War Diary	Sovilla	01/03/1918	12/03/1918
War Diary	Gezaincourt	13/03/1917	20/03/1917
War Diary	Contay	21/03/1918	21/03/1918
War Diary	Ablainyzeville	22/03/1918	22/03/1918
War Diary	Favreuil	22/03/1918	26/03/1918
War Diary	Essarts	26/03/1917	28/03/1917
War Diary	Hannescamps	29/03/1918	31/03/1918
War Diary	Hannescamps	01/04/1918	14/04/1918
War Diary	Gommecourt	14/04/1918	27/04/1918
War Diary	Chau De La Haie	28/04/1918	30/04/1918
War Diary	Pas	01/05/1918	09/05/1918
War Diary		08/05/1918	12/05/1918
War Diary	Pas	12/05/1918	16/05/1918
War Diary	H6b 25.55	17/05/1918	31/05/1918
War Diary	I6 b 3.5	01/06/1918	03/06/1918
War Diary	I 5a 0.5.85	03/06/1918	07/06/1918
War Diary	Eringhem	08/06/1918	10/06/1918
War Diary	Muncq Nieurliet	11/06/1918	25/06/1918
War Diary	Eringhem	26/06/1918	30/06/1918
War Diary	27/L14.d 00.95	01/07/1918	01/07/1918
War Diary	28/G 33a 85.05	02/07/1918	10/07/1918
War Diary	G 33d 65.60	11/07/1918	31/07/1918
Miscellaneous	41st Division "A"	03/09/1918	03/09/1918
War Diary	G 33d 65.60	01/08/1918	15/08/1918
War Diary		14/08/1918	17/08/1918
War Diary	27/K22a 9.7.	18/08/1918	31/08/1918
War Diary	G 33 d 65.60	01/09/1918	01/09/1918
War Diary	M 6 C 3.4	01/09/1918	04/09/1918
War Diary	M 7 C 2.2	04/09/1918	07/09/1918
War Diary	H 8 C 6.1.	08/09/1918	11/09/1918
War Diary	H. 27b. 6.7.	12/09/1918	28/09/1918
War Diary	I 26d. 4.3	12/09/1918	30/09/1918
War Diary	O6b	01/10/1918	01/10/1918

Type	Location	Start	End
War Diary	J 36.d.0.0	01/10/1918	03/10/1918
War Diary	J 29 b.7.2.	04/10/1918	14/10/1918
War Diary	K 30 C 6.0	14/10/1918	15/10/1918
War Diary	K 28a. 95.03	16/10/1918	17/10/1918
War Diary	L 17d 8.2	17/10/1918	20/10/1918
War Diary	N 2b. 45.95	21/10/1918	21/10/1918
War Diary	H 34 C 5.5.	21/10/1918	21/10/1918
War Diary	O.1.c.9.4	21/10/1918	29/10/1918
War Diary	P.25C 35.35.	30/10/1918	31/10/1918
Miscellaneous	Headquarters, 41st. Division "A".		
War Diary	Sheet 4 1/100.000 4 K 23.78.	01/12/1918	22/12/1918
War Diary	Vieux Waleffe	23/12/1918	31/12/1918
War Diary	Vieux Waleffe	01/01/1919	01/01/1919
War Diary	East of Liege	02/01/1919	31/01/1919
Miscellaneous	Headquarters, 41st Division "A"	28/02/1919	28/02/1919
War Diary	Wahn Barracks SE. of Cologne	01/02/1919	01/02/1919
War Diary	Deutz-Cologne	02/02/1919	28/02/1919
Miscellaneous	London Division G	02/05/1919	02/05/1919
War Diary	Cologne Germany	01/04/1919	12/05/1919
War Diary	Cologne Deutz Germany	13/05/1919	29/10/1919

41ST DIVISION

190TH BRIGADE R.F.A.

MAY 1916 - ~~DEC 1918~~. OCT 1917
MAR 1918 - 1919 OCT

ITALY 1917 NOV - 1918 FEB

2625

WO 95/2625/5
41 DIV
190 BDE RFA   May 1916 – Oct 1917

Army Form C. 2118.

190 R.F.A
Vol 1

WAR DIARY
or
INTELLIGENCE SUMMARY
(Erase heading not required.)

Place	Date	Hour	Summary of Events and Information	Remarks and references to Appendices
			May	
HAVRE	5-5-16	10.30 A.M	Disembarked and proceeded to Rest Camp	
HAVRE	6-5-16	9.30 PM	Entrained and proceeded to STEENBECQUE and thence by road to PRADELLES via HAZEBROUCK 7/5/16	
PRADELLES	7-5-16	1.30 PM	Arrived. Took over action and remained until 27/5/16	
PRADELLES	27-5-16	4.30	One Section "C" Battery relieved remaining detachments of 52nd Brigade R.F.A	
PRADELLES		10 PM	One Section "C" Battery returned to billets	
PRADELLES	28-5-16	Noon	Relieved 52nd Brigade R.F.A taking over their guns and positions also their quarters.	

M[signature]
Lt. Col. R.F.A.
Comdg. 190th (Wimbledon) Bde. R.F.A.

41 JUNE
190 R.F.A.
Vol 2

WAR DIARY
or
INTELLIGENCE SUMMARY

Army Form C. 2118

(Erase heading not required.)

Place	Date	Hour	Summary of Events and Information	Remarks and references to Appendices
In the Field	10/6/16 to 17/6	1.30 pm to 2.30 am	Gas Attack by the enemy	
	17/6/16		2 Lieutenants G. H. Parry R.F.A. reported his arrival and was posted to "A" Battery. 90th Brigade R.F.A.	
	30/6/16		2/Lieutenants E. J. Lort R.F.A. reported his arrival and was posted to "D" Battery. 183rd Brigade R.F.A.	
	1/6 to 30/6/16		During this period Batteries carried out routine operations from their positions and fired 4,500 rounds.	

[signature]
Lt. Col. R.F.A.
Comdg. 190th (Wimbledon) Bde. R.F.A.

WAR DIARY
or
INTELLIGENCE SUMMARY   190 Bde RFA

Army Form C. 2118

Place	Date	Hour	Summary of Events and Information	Remarks and references to Appendices
In the Field	1/7/16		2/Lt. A.H. Andrew reported his arrival and was posted to B/190	
			2/Lt. R.M. Marians " " " " " " B/183	
	1/7/16	3 A.M.	A/190 fired 40 Rds on Hostile Trenches at request of Infantry	
		3.15 PM	C/190 " 32 " " Suspected O.Pos FUZE COTTAGE U.10.a.2.3 (Map 28 S.W.)	
		11.0 AM	D/190 (How) 40 " " MONASTERY at U.24.c.6.9 with good results	
	2/7/16	7.10 AM	A/190 – silenced a H.T.M. in action at U.16.a.2.2.	
			C/190 – fired 28 Rds at Suspected O.P – Several direct hits	
			D/190 – carried out a shoot with K.B.S. on SPINNING MILL at U.15 Central and TRIG. WIE ART at U.15.c.2.0.	
	3/7/16	8.30 PM to 12.0 Mdt	Batteries of Left Group carried out a shoot according to Divisional Orders on Enem Roads.	
	3/7/16	12.30 PM 1.45 PM	B/183 & D/183 retaliated on Enemy Batteries for hostile shelling of road R PETIT PONT – HYDE PARK CORNER.	
		12.15 PM	A/190 fired at Enemy's support trench to silence hostile M.G. fire on our aeroplanes flying low over our line.	
	4/7/16		A/190 retaliated on Enemy's Communication Trench for hostile shelling by T.M.	
			B/183 fired 40 Rds at FACTORY FARM U.15.d.92.3. with good Results	
			D/190 carried out a shoot with K.B.S. on SWISS CHALET CHATEAU U.12.d.4.2	
	5/7/16	5.30 PM to 7.30 PM	Batteries retaliated on Enemy Trench Motors with good results	
	6/7/16		Batteries registered various targets.	

WAR DIARY or INTELLIGENCE SUMMARY

Army Form C. 2118

(Erase heading not required.)

Instructions regarding War Diaries and Intelligence Summaries are contained in F.S. Regs., Part II. and the Staff Manual respectively. Title Pages will be prepared in manuscript.

Place	Date	Hour	Summary of Events and Information	Remarks and references to Appendices
In the Field	7/7/16	8.30 AM	2/Lt. E.R. Bartlett reported his arrival and was posted to D/190	
		5 PM	All Batteries 18 Pr. carried out shoot for cutting wire for support of Infantry in minor operations. Howitzer Batteries fired at Enemy's communication trenches and support trenches	
	8/7/16	9.30 AM	All Batteries 18 Pr. carried out shoot for cutting wire in cooperation with Infantry in Minor Operation. Howitzer Batteries fired at Hostile Trench Mortars in cooperation with Infantry	
	9/7/16	10 PM to 12.0 PM	Batteries fired at Communication & Support Trenches in cooperation with Infantry in minor Operation.	
	10/7/16		Registration of targets by Batteries.	
	11/7/16	1-0 AM to 1.25 AM	B/183 } Fired at Enemy hostile Trenches – Dornonine Grendon Cole A/190 }	
			A/190, B/190, C/190. Fired at Enemy Support Trenches, to silence Hostile M.G. fire on our Aeroplane flying low.	
	11/7/16	10 PM	C/183 remove their gun from T.18.C.2.5 to T.24.C.12.9 in order to operate with Left groups and B/183 moved to Centre Group.	
	12/7/16	Lepois Dug. 6.30 AM	Batteries carried out shoot for cutting wire in cooperation with Infantry in minor Operation. C/183 were heavily shelled in their new position. Captain Hayman 2/Lt W.E. Hanyer and 2/Lt. J. Field of C/183 and 5 O.R. were wounded. One gun being put out of action.	

1875 Wt. W593/826 1,000,000 4/15 J.B.C. & A. A.D.S.S./Forms/C. 2118.

WAR DIARY
or
INTELLIGENCE SUMMARY

(Erase heading not required.)

Army Form C. 2118

Instructions regarding War Diaries and Intelligence Summaries are contained in F.S. Regs., Part II. and the Staff Manual respectively. Title Pages will be prepared in manuscript.

Place	Date	Hour	Summary of Events and Information	Remarks and references to Appendices
In the Field	12/7/16	5.30 PM	2/Lt. P.J. Elkins reported his arrival and was posted to C/190	AA
			2/Lt. F.J. Norton " " " " D/190	AA
			2/Lt. E.J. Coe " " " " C/183	AA
			2/Lt. W.H. Felstead " " " " C/183	AA
			2/Lt. H.E.E. Hunt " " " " D/183	AA
	13/7/16		Registration of Targets by Batteries.	AA
	14/7/16		Batteries fired on Enemy. Enemy rather quiet in Minor Operations. Howitzer Batteries Retaliated on Enemy's Trench Mortars	AA AA
	15/7/16	5D PM	A/190 fired on Hostile Trench Mortars with good effect. Batteries fired on Hostile Support Trenches in cooperation with Infantry in minor operations.	AA AA
	16/7/16	12 NOON	Colonel C.E. Stewart RFA took over command of O.P's Colonel W.H. Connolly RFA took over command of Left Group.	AA AA

Army Form C. 2118.

WAR DIARY
or
INTELLIGENCE SUMMARY
(Erase heading not required.)

Instructions regarding War Diaries and Intelligence Summaries are contained in F. S. Regs., Part II. and the Staff Manual respectively. Title Pages will be prepared in manuscript.

Place	Date	Hour	Summary of Events and Information	Remarks and references to Appendices
In the field	July 14th	17-20	Visited all O.P.s handed over by Colonel Connolly R.F.A.	
	15th		Visited O.P. at Ploegsteert Wood and superintended the construction	
	16th		Visited O.P. at Le Vale Cottage and superintended the construction	
	20th		Visited O.P. at S2 and superintended the construction	
	21st		Visited O.P. at Le Vale Cottage and superintended the construction	
	22nd		Visited O.P. at Ploegsteert	
	23rd		Visited Hill 63 and looked for new site for O.P.	
	24th		Visited Hill 63 and looked for new site for O.P. ditto	
	25th			
	26th		Visited O.P. at Ploegsteert Wood	
	27th		O.P. at Ploegsteert Wood finally completed	
	28th		O.P at CHATEAU LA HUTTE visited and selected site for new O.P.	
	29th		Visited LEGHEER O.P. with a view to lengthening same	
	30th		Visited site for O.P. at Carter Farm	
	31st		Visited S2 & Le Vale Cottage and superintended the construction	

Lt. M. McCaffery
Comdg. 190th (Wimbledon) Bde. R.F.A.

WAR DIARY or INTELLIGENCE SUMMARY

Army Form C. 2118

190 Bde R.F.A.

Vol 4

Place	Date	Hour	Summary of Events and Information	Remarks and references to Appendices
In the Field	1/8/16		Visited O.P. on Hill 63 and superintended construction	WD
	2/8/16		Visited O.P. on Hill 63 do	WD
	3/8/16		Visited LE VALE COT. O.P. and O.P. at S2 123 and superintended construction ditto	WD
	4/8/16		ditto	WD
	5/8/16		Visited MACHINE GUN HOUSE and superintended strengthening of same	WD
	6/8/16		SUNDAY – REST DAY	WD
	7/8/16		Visited O.P's at LE VALE COT., S2 123 and HILL 63	WD
	8/8/16		Visited O.P's at LE VALE COT., S2 123, HILL 63 and Alhambra O.P. (further addition of masonry)	WD
	9/8/16		Visited O.P's at LE VALE COT, S2 123	WD
	10/8/16		O.P's at LE VALE COT and S2 123 completed. Strengthening of O.P at MACHINE GUN HOUSE proceeded with.	
	11/8/16		Advised in the removal of a hut so an aeroplane field for the purpose of reconstruction into use as a church. The church at NIEPPE having been destroyed	WD
	12/8/16		Lt. Col. C.E. Steward R.F.A Commanding 190th Bde R.F.A visited IV.th Army Corps Headquarters on the SOMME.	WD
	13/8/16		REST DAY – The D.A.C. men attached to the Brigade for O.P work returned to their Unit	WD
	14/8/16		Lieutenant C.T. Ferrie R.F.A Orderly Officer transferred to "A" Battery. 2nd Lieutenant W.U. Squire R.F.A H Battery appointed Orderly Officer.	WD

1875 W.: W 593/326 1,000,000 4/15 J.B.C. & A. A.D.S.S./Forms/C. 2118.

Army Form C. 2118

WAR DIARY
or
INTELLIGENCE SUMMARY
(Erase heading not required.)

Instructions regarding War Diaries and Intelligence Summaries are contained in F.S. Regs., Part II. and the Staff Manual respectively. Title Pages will be prepared in manuscript.

Place	Date	Hour	Summary of Events and Information	Remarks and references to Appendices
In the Field	15/8/16		Lieut J.S.B. Ridge R.F.A. Adjutant 190th Bde R.F.A. proceeded to BAILLEUL AND EECKE with Interpreter as Billeting Officer.	WmE
	16/8/16		Prepare for move to the SOMME Area.	WmE
	17/8/16		ditto	WmE
	18/8/16		ditto	WmE
	19/8/16		ditto	WmE
	20/8/16		Right Half Sections of Batteries were relieved by batteries of the 23rd Divisional Artillery and moved to BAILLEUL Reserve Area. & ABBEVILLE appointed/proceeded	WmE
	21/8/16		Remainder of Brigade relieved by 23rd Divisional Artillery, left Sections moving to BAILLEUL reserve area and Brigade Headquarters to EECKE.	WmE
	22/8/16		Submitted Programme of Drill in new training area at SOMME.	WmE
	23/8/16		2/Lieutenant L. Hill reported his arrival and was posted to A/190 2/Lieutenant L. Humphrys reported his arrival and was posted to B/190	WmE
	24/8/16	4:13 AM	Brigade Headquarters entrained at BAILLEUL WEST STATION for ABBEVILLE GOEDVERSWELDE for PONT REMY	
		9:38 AM	A/190 entrained at BAILLEUL " " PONT REMY	
		12:38 PM	B/190 " " " " PONT REMY	
		3:38 PM	C/190 " " " " PONT REMY	
		6:38 PM	D/190 " " " " PONT REMY	WmE

Army Form C. 2118

WAR DIARY
or
INTELLIGENCE SUMMARY
(Erase heading not required.)

Instructions regarding War Diaries and Intelligence Summaries are contained in F.S. Regs., Part II. and the Staff Manual respectively. Title Pages will be prepared in manuscript.

Place	Date	Hour	Summary of Events and Information	Remarks and references to Appendices
In the Field	24/8/16	3.20 PM	Brigade H.Q. arrived at ABBEVILLE and at 3.15 P.M. proceeded to Billets at L'ETOILE, which were reached at 6.30 P.M. Batteries arrived at PONT REMY and at once proceeded to Billets at L'ETOILE. Inspection and cleaning of BILLETS.	WS
	25/8/16		Inspection and cleaning of BILLETS.	WS
	26/8/16		Training commenced. DRILL ORDER.	WS
	27/8/16		SUNDAY. Church Parade. Inspection and Harness cleaning	WS
	28/8/16		Inspection of Guns taken over from relieving Batteries by I.O.M. Training in Drill Order continued. Visual Signalling & lectures by O.C. Batteries	WS
	29/8/16		ROUTE MARCH. Ranging marches and manoeuvres.	WS
	30/8/16		ROUTE MARCH. Practised taking up positions and supply of ammunition by B.A.C.	WS
	31/8/16		Inspection of teams for Divisional Horse Show. Lieut Col C.E. Stewart accompanied by 6 Officers of the Brigade visited the Somme battlefield. Lieut Col C.E. Stewart. (killed) 2/Lieut W.D Squire - Orderly Officer wounded	WS

William N. Sauer
Major R.A.
Cmdg 190 Bde RFA

Army Form C. 2118

190 RFA
Vol 5

WAR DIARY
INTELLIGENCE SUMMARY
(Erase heading not required.)

Place	Date	Hour	Summary of Events and Information	Remarks and references to Appendices
L'ÉTOILE	Sept 1st 1916	4:30 a.m.	Orders received for the Brigade to be ready to move off at 9 P.M. the same day. About midnight news had come in that Lt Col STEWART had been killed near MAMETZ on the previous day whilst going round battery positions, 2nd Lt DW. SQUIRE Orderly Officer was wounded at the same time.	
		1 P.M.	Major WICKHAM sent from A/183 to command the Brigade temporarily	
		9 P.M.	Brigade left L'ÉTOILE and marched to LONG PRÉ via FLIXECOURT - BELLOY-SUR-SOMME - LACHAUSSÉE - ST SAUVEUR	
LONGPRÉ	2.9.16	2 a.m.	Arrived at LONGPRÉ	
		2 P.M.	Orders received to continue the march that night and go to DERNANCOURT.	
		8:40 PM	Brigade moved off and marched to DERNANCOURT via AMIENS and QUERRIEU	
DERNANCOURT	3.9.16	5 a.m.	Arrived at DERNANCOURT and bivouaced there. Lt J. RIDGE posted to A/190 Lt CFFAVIELL took over Adjutant Lt.COL. G.A. CARDEN posted to the Brigade and took over command. Lt. J. RIDGE posted from A/190 to Ammunition Dump O.C. Brigade and battery Commanders went forward and reconnoitred positions in the vicinity of BAZENTIN LE GRAND. Working parties from the batteries came up later and started preparing positions.	
	4.9.16			
	5.9.16		Work continued on positions.	
BAZENTIN LE GRAND	6.9.16		Batteries moved up and came into action by dawn. Positions about 1000x NE of BAZENTIN-LE-GRAND. Bde HQ in BAZENTIN-LE-GRAND Wood.	
	7.9.16			
	8.9.16		No firing done. Batteries continued to improve positions. Major W.N. SAWER attached to 41st FA, HQ. Capt J.C. Callaghan M.C. posted to command C/190. Casualties 1.O.R. Killed 2.O.Rs Wounded.	
	9.9.16		B/190 and C/190 started registering - 8 rounds fired. Casualties 4.O.Rs Wounded.	

Army Form C. 2118

WAR DIARY or INTELLIGENCE SUMMARY

(Erase heading not required.)

Instructions regarding War Diaries and Regs., Part II.
Summary Staff Manual respectively. Title Pages
will be prepared in manuscript.

Place	Date	Hour	Summary of Events and Information	Remarks and references to Appendices
DAZENTIN -LE-GRAND.	10.9.16		Batteries continued registering points in their zone. 88 rounds fired. Casualties 9 O.R. wounded. 2nd Lt F.M.V.EARLE posted to C/190.	
	11.9.16		From 12 noon on this day 41st D.A. became responsible for the close defence of the line. Orders received during the evening that the preliminary bombardment would start on the following day & last for three days. Casualties 1 O.R. killed 6 O.R. wounded. 538 rounds fired during the day.	
	12.9.16		Preliminary bombardment started at 6 am. on all the enemy defences and approaches within range. SWITCH LINE and FLERS and approaches to FLERS engaged. 1586 rds 18 Pr and 452 rds 4.5" How fired during the day. Casualties 2nd Lt. C.A. LOUGHMAN slightly wounded.	
	13.9.16		Bombardment continued as on previous day. 1164 rds 18 Pr fired and 251 rds 4.5" Hows. Casualties. NIL.	
	14.9.16		Bombardment continued all day as before. Special objective were, TEA SUPPORT and SWITCH LINE. 2nd Lt. C.A. LOUGHMAN returned to D/190 to duty. 2065 rds 18 Pr fired and 858 rds 4.5" Hows. Casualties 1 O.R. killed and 2 O.R. wounded.	
	15.9.16	6.20am	Zero hour. Batteries barraged. B/190 formed creeping barrage and A/190 stationary barrage. D/190 bombarded the Southern road and approaches to FLERS. C/190 had been previously detailed as counter battery under the orders of O.C. Counter batteries XV Corps.	
		10.40am	B/190 ceased fire	
		11.20am	D/190 " "	
		11.50am	A/190 " "	
		3.15 PM	A Message received from 41st D.A. to the effect that the enemy were massing 1000 x N of FLERS. A/190 & B/190 immediately started a barrage across this line & D/190 shelled the sunken road 100 x due north of FLERS. This was continued (but no attack developed) until at	
		4.30 PM	Orders were received to start cutting wire on the GIRD Trench.	

Army Form C. 2118.

WAR DIARY
INTELLIGENCE SUMMARY
(Erase heading not required.)

Instructions regarding War Diaries and Intelligence Summaries are contained in F. S. Regs., Part II. and the Staff Manual respectively. Title Pages will be prepared in manuscript.

Place	Date	Hour	Summary of Events and Information	Remarks and references to Appendices
BAZENTIN LE-GRAND.	15.9.16	7 PM	Orders received to reconnoitre forward position in rear of FLERS. Owing to failing light, this had to be postponed until the morning. Casualties 2/Lt. C.A. LOUGHMAN. wounded, 1 OR wounded. 498 rds of 18 Pr & 616 rds 4·5" How' fired during the day.	
NEAR LONGUEVAL	16.9.16	5 am	O.C. Brigade went forward and selected positions in the valley north of LONGUEVAL.	
		11 am	O.C. Brigade took O.C. up allotted positions work was immediately started, platforms & ammunition Dumps being made. The former was very necessary because the ground was so cut up by shell fire. Batteries moved up during the afternoon and registered most important points by dusk. C/190 remained in its original position, being still under the orders of O.C. XV Corps Counter Batteries. A/189 and D/189 came into Group commanded by LT. COL. G.A. CAIDEW. 2328 rds 18 Pr & 308 rds 4·5" How's fired. Casualties - NIL.	
	17.9.16		At dawn batteries started cutting wire on GIRD. LINE.	
		10 am	Orders received to stop wire cutting and to carry out a slow deliberate bombardment all day night on all hostile works and approaches etc within range in the Brigade Zone. This zone was now about 400° wide running approx'ly N.E. & S.W. through the West edge of GUEUDECOURT. During the evening C/190 took over A/189's position. A/189 & D/169 going back under the command of O.C. Bag Ode. 4160 rds 18 Pr & 720 rds 4·5" How's fired. Casualties 1/2 OR wounded.	
	18.9.16		Ordinary day firing carried out from 6·30 am to 6·30 pm, as ordered. Rained most part of the day making the ground very heavy & difficult for transport. 957 rds 18 Pr & 194 rds 4·5 How's fired. Casualties 1 OR. Wounded.	

Army Form C. 2118

WAR DIARY

INTELLIGENCE SUMMARY

(Erase heading not required.)

Instructions regarding War Diaries and Intelligence Summaries are contained in F. S. Regs., Part II. and the Staff Manual respectively. Title Pages will be prepared in manuscript.

Place	Date	Hour	Summary of Events and Information	Remarks and references to Appendices
NEAR LONGUEVAL	19.9.16		Ordinary day and night bombardment carried out as before. 55 rnds 18 Pr. and 65 rnds 4·5" How fired. Casualties Capt W.J. MORLEY evacuated - shell shock. 2 O.R. wounded. Weather still bad.	
	20.9.16		Ordinary day and night bombardment carried out 526 rnds 18 Pr. and 59 rnds 4·5 How fired. Casualties NIL	
	21.9.16		Ordinary bombardment. Orders received for a fresh attack on 23rd inst, bombardment to start at 4 am following morning. 573 rnds 18 Pr fired & 140 rnds 4·5" How. Casualties - NIL. Weather conditions still bad. 2/Lt E.R. BARTLETT D/190 evacuated sick.	
	22.9.16	2 am	Orders for bombardment & attack postponed. Ordinary day firing carried on. 69 rnds 18 pr fired & 110 rnds 4·5 How. Capt. S.A. FERRIER posted to command A/190. Casualties / nil./	
	23.9.16		Ordinary day & night firing 441 rnds 18 pr & 159 rnds 4·5" How fired. Casualties 4 O.R. killed 16 O.R. wounded. 2/Lt J.B.A. Simpart evacuated sick. 2/Lt L.A. DENT. posted in his place to D/190.	
	24.9.16	7 am	Preparatory bombardment began. All points of importance in rear of the enemy's lines coming under the special attention was paid to CARD TRENCH. GIRD. SUPPORT and the vicinity of SEVEN DIALS and GUEUDECOURT. VILLAGE. Bombardment continued till 6·30 pm when ordinary night firing started. 1095 rnds 18 pr and 230 rnds 4·5" Hows fired. Casualties 6 OR wounded. 2/Lt C.K. EXLEY posted to D/190.	
	25.9.16	6·30 am	Bombardment started again.	

1875 Wt. W593/826 1,000,000 4/15 J.B.C. & A. A.D.S.S./Forms/C. 2118.

Army Form C. 2118.

WAR DIARY
INTELLIGENCE SUMMARY
(Erase heading not required.)

Instructions regarding War Diaries and Intelligence Summaries are contained in F. S. Regs., Part II. and the Staff Manual respectively. Title Pages will be prepared in manuscript.

Place	Date	Hour	Summary of Events and Information	Remarks and references to Appendices
NEAR LONGUEVAL	25.9.16	12.35pm	Zero hour. Batteries formed part of the Stationary barrage C/90 covering the whole Dele Zone & being ready to engage any favourable target. GUEUDECOURT was captured. 917 rds 18 pr fired and 367 rds 4.5" hows. Casualties 1. OR killed 8. OR wounded.	
	26.9.16		Ordinary day firing. 1083 rds 18 pr & 365 rds 4.5" hows fired. Casualties 2/Lt A.K. ANDREWS wounded. 11 ORs Wounded.	
	27.9.16	3.15pm	Bombardment of GIRD. LINE, during the morning in preparation for a small attack to be launched in the afternoon. Zero hour. Infantry attacked a small portion of the GIRD. LINE and GIRD SUPPORT and captured. Batteries formed a creeping barrage. 3065 rds 18 pr and 578 rds 4.5" hows fired. Casualties. NIL.	
	28.9.16		Ordinary day firing. New positions reconnoitred. West and N.W of FLERS. Ordered by D.A. to stand worth to these and have one registering Gun in position by dawn 30th 16yrds 18 pr and 363 rds 4.5" hows fired. Casualties Capt. G.R. JENKINS. evacuated sick. Capt R.H.A. LOVE posted to command D/90. 2/Lt. S.R. METGE and 2/Lt. C.C.P. TURNER. posted to C/90. 1.O.R. killed and 1.O.R. Wounded	

Army Form C. 2118

WAR DIARY
INTELLIGENCE SUMMARY
(Erase heading not required.)

Place	Date	Hour	Summary of Events and Information	Remarks and references to Appendices
NEAR LONGUEVAL	29.9.16		Ordinary day firing. Work begun on new forward position. Single gun now has to be un-acted by team. Wct 3rd 1195 rds 18Prs and 294 rds 4.5 show fired. Casualties 2/Lt M.V. ROWE wounded. 2/Lt E.J. CASTELLO posted to C/190. 1 O.R. wounded	
	30.9.16		Ordinary day firing. 896 rds 18 Pr & 315 rds 4.5 Hows fired. Casualties 2/Lt J.E. CHAMBERS wounded.	

Signed
C/O 190 Bde RFA

Lt D.C.
Army Form C. 2118

WAR DIARY
or
INTELLIGENCE SUMMARY
(Erase heading not required.)

190 Bde RFA

Place	Date	Hour	Summary of Events and Information	Remarks and references to Appendices
LONGUEVAL	1.10.16		Normal day and night firing carried out. Work continued on forward positions near FLERS. Casualties - 2/Lieut. A.W. HALL wounded. Amm. expended, 18Pr., 1547rds, 4.5"How, 302rds.	
	2.10.16		Normal day and night firing carried out. Weather conditions much improved. Casualties - 2/Lieut. J. BOWDEN, A/190, 2/Lieut. T.R.S. PARRY, A/190 and 6 O.R. Amm expended 583 18Pr. and 210 4.5" How.	
	3.10.16		Normal day and night firing carried out. Orders received to have the one Section in action in the new positions by dawn Oct 6th and the others by dawn Oct. 7th. Casualties nil. Ammunition expended 18Pr., 780 rds., and 4.5"How 146 rds.	
	4.10.16		No operations. Normal firing. Ammunition expended - 18Pr. 557 rds., and 4.5"How. 299 rds. Casualties nil.	
	5.10.16		Normal conditions. Ammunition expended 18Pr. 685 rds., 4.5"How 123 rds. Casualties 2 O.R.	
	6.10.16		One Section per battery came into action at dawn in the forward positions on the FLERS - EAUCOURT-ABBAYE road at M30c. and acquired. D/190's position in rear of 18Pr's and just behind FLERS. Casualties 2 O.R's wounded. Ammunition expended 1223 rds. 18Pr. 426 rds 4.5" How.	
Near FLERS	7.10.16		Remaining Sections and H.Q's were up at the new positions by dawn. Attack along the front at 2.20 p.m. (Zero hour). A/190 and B/190's assisted in forming creeping barrage C/190 and stationary respectively. C/190 had one Section on each. The attack was a failure, the infantry reporting that they were held up by m/c gun fire. Casualties 1 O.R. wounded. Ammunition expended 1760 rds 18Pr and 236 rds. 4.5" How.	

Army Form C. 2118

WAR DIARY
or
INTELLIGENCE SUMMARY
(Erase heading not required.)

Instructions regarding War Diaries and Intelligence Summaries are contained in F. S. Regs., Part II and the Staff Manual respectively. Title Pages will be prepared in manuscript.

Place	Date	Hour	Summary of Events and Information	Remarks and references to Appendices
Near FLERS	8.10.16		Normal firing and conditions again. Casualties - 0/Lt. S.J.C MELVILLE, A/190 wounded. Ammunition expended. R.F.A. 835 rds, 4.5" How. 82 rds.	
	9.10.16		Normal firing during day and night. Ammunition expended 1622 rds. 8/18 Pr. and 263 rds 4.5" How. Casualties, nil.	2/Lieut. P.R. BOYLE posted to A/190
	10.10.16		First day of a two day bombardment gun in preparation & for operations on Oct. 12th. 18 Pr. Battaries dealt with any enemy left in front of BAYONET TRENCH and SCABBARD TRENCH in the Brigade zone, also bombarded BARLEY TRENCH. 4.5 How. on these trenches. Ammunition expended 1243 rds. 18 Pr., 199 rds. of 4.5" How.. Casualties 1 O.R. wounded.	
	11.12.16		Bombardment continued. At 3.40 p.m. there was a Chinese bombardment along the whole front. 1430 rds. 18 Pr. & 455 rds. 4.5" How. fired during the day. Casualties 2 O.R. wounded.	
	12.10.16	2-3 p.m.	Continued bombardment during the morning Zero hour. B/190 and C/190 formed part of a creeping barrage. A/190 fired a LUISENHOF FARM, until the barrage reached then, when they joined it. D/190 put up a barrage of gas shell in rear. The attack was not successful. Infantry on own immediate report night being held up by enemy. Ammunition expended 2460 rds. 18 P., 5160 rds. 4.5" How, and 330 Gas. Casualties 3 O.R. wounded.	

WAR DIARY or INTELLIGENCE SUMMARY

Army Form C. 2118

Place	Date	Hour	Summary of Events and Information	Remarks and references to Appendices
near FLERS	13.10.16		Normal day firing. Ammunition expended 836 rds. 18 Pr. and 244 rds. 4.5" How.	
	14.10.16		From 12.30 a.m. to 3 a.m. battery position and H.Q. heavily shelled with gas shells (phosgene). No casualties were sustained however. At 2.15 there was a bombardment of the whole front by heavy artillery. 18 Pr. batteries assisted by shelling BAYONET TRENCH. Ammunition expended 1319 rds. 18 Pr. and 255 rds. 4.5" How. Casualties, 2/Lieut. C.K. EXLEY wounded, and 3 O.R.	
	15.10.16		Normal day firing except for a small bombardment of BAYONET TRENCH at 3.15 p.m. in which all batteries of the brigade took part in conjunction with the heavy artillery. B/190 heavily shelled during the afternoon, some material damage was done but no casualties. Ammunition expended: 10110 rds. 18 Pr., 355 rds. 4.5" How. Casualties, 1 O.R.	
	16.10.16		18 Pr. batteries assisted in shelling any existing wire on Bde. front in front of BAYONET TRENCH. Ammunition 995 rds. 18 Pr., 203 rds. 4.5" How. Casualties nil.	
	17.10.16		Normal firing during the day. Special attention being paid to any existing mobile wire. Ammunition expended 729 rds. 18 Pr. and 176 rds. 4.5" How.	
	18.10.16		A local attack at 3.40 a.m. (German hour). The objectives were small portions of trench on our immediate right. No advance on the Brigade front. All go forward part of the standing	

WAR DIARY or INTELLIGENCE SUMMARY

Army Form C. 2118

(Erase heading not required.)

Place	Date	Hour	Summary of Events and Information	Remarks and references to Appendices
Area FLERS	18.10.16		Barrage and B/190 and C/190 the creeping barrage. D/190 was at this time under XV Corps Counter Battery. Objectives was reached, but it was found impossible to hold them. Remainder of the day normal firing. Ammunition expended 2317 rds 18 Pr and 425 rds 4.5" How. Casualties nil.	
	19.10.16		Normal day firing. Ammunition expended 780 rds 18 Pr and 208 rds 4.5" How. Casualties nil.	
	20.10.16		Normal day firing. C/190 heavily shelled during the afternoon causing some material damage and several casualties. Ammunition expended 830 rds 18 Pr and 159 rds 4.5" How. Casualties 8 O.R. wounded.	
	21.10.16		Normal day firing. Batteries received an S.O.S. at about 4.30 p.m. from the infantry, but this proved to be nothing more than a heavy bombardment of our front by the enemy. No actual assault. Ammunition expended – 887 rds 18 Pr. and 190 rds 4.5" How. Casualties 8 O.R. wounded, 2 O.R. killed.	
	22.10.16		Orders received for a general attack along the whole front, to capture BAYONET TRENCH, BARLEY TRENCH and LIME TRENCH, Reserve Army and Trench army to cooperate on the left and right respectively. The attack became "G" in Oct. Normal day firing. Ammunition expended – 371 rds 18 Pr and 190 rds 4.5" How. Casualties nil.	

WAR DIARY or INTELLIGENCE SUMMARY

Army Form C. 2118

Place	Date	Hour	Summary of Events and Information	Remarks and references to Appendices
Near FLERS	23.10.16		Normal day firing. Attack for 24th postponed. Owing to continuous bad weather this attack was postponed indefinitely, and did not eventually take place until after the 41st B.A. were relieved. Ammunition expended 806 rds. 18Pr. and 168 rds. 4.5" How. Casualties 1 O.R. (wounded)	
	24.10.16		Normal firing during day and night. Ammunition expended 626 rds. 18Pr. and 165 rds. 4.5" How.	
	25.10.16		Normal day and night firing. Ammunition expended 579 rds. 18Pr. and 162 rds. 4.5" How. Casualties 4 O.R. hit, 1 died of wounds and one wounded.	
	26.10.16		From 12.30 a.m. to 4.30 a.m. 18Pr Batteries were heavily shelled with gas shell, tear gas and phosgene. Resulting in some material damage and several casualties. Normal day & night firing during the remainder of the 24 hours. Ammunition expended 639 rds. 18Pr. and 200 rds. 4.5" How. Casualties 2 Lt. HAA Ballain [?] and admitted to hospital. 2 OR. died of gas poisoning, 4 O.R. admitted to hospital suffering from gas, 7 O.R. wounded.	
	27.10.16		Normal day and night firing. Ammunition expended 463 rds. 18Pr. and 138 rds. 4.5" How. Casualties 1 O.R. wounded.	
	28.10.16		Normal day & night firing. Received orders that the B.A. were to be relieved on 29/30 and 30/31st. Ammunition expended 729 rds. 18Pr. and 156 4.5" How. Casualties nil	
	29.10.16		Normal day firing. Col. Watts commanding 4 Bde AFA came up to H.Q. to take over. Ammunition expended 687 rds. 18Pr. and 150 rds. 4.5" How. Casualties 1 O.R. wounded.	
	30.10.16		Normal day firing. One section per battery went back to the wagon lines and their places taken by sections from 4 Bde. AFA. Ammunition expended 503 rds. 18Pr. & 150 rds. 4.5" How.	

Army Form C. 2118

WAR DIARY or INTELLIGENCE SUMMARY

(Erase heading not required.)

190* Brigade
R.F.A
Vol 6

Place	Date	Hour	Summary of Events and Information	Remarks and references to Appendices
Near FLERS	31.10.16		Remaining Sections and H.Q. were relieved during the day and went down to the waggon lines near LONGUEVAL. The sections which were relieved yesterday left for BONNAY at 9 a.m. Casualties, 3 O.R's wounded.	

Army Form C. 2118

190 Bde RFA

WAR DIARY
INTELLIGENCE SUMMARY
(Erase heading not required.)

Instructions regarding War Diaries and Intelligence Summaries are contained in F.S. Regs., Part II. and the Staff Manual respectively. Title Pages will be prepared in manuscript.

Vol 7

Place	Date	Hour	Summary of Events and Information	Remarks and references to Appendices
LONGUEVAL	1.11.16	6.30 am	The Brigade moved out of the wagon lines and marched to billets at BONNAY via CARNOY - MAMETZ - DERNANCOURT - HEILLY The CRA having proceeded on leave of absence Lt-Col Cardew took over command of the D.A. and Capt AHAD LOVE the Brigade.	
BONNAY		4.30 pm	Arrived into billets at BONNAY.	
"	2.11.16		Rested at BONNAY.	
"	3.11.16	6.30 pm	The Brigade marched from BONNAY to MOULLIENS.	
MOULLIENS		12.15	Arrived in billets at MOULLIENS.	
"	4.11.16	7.10am	Brigade moved out of MOULLIENS and marched to AMPLIERS via PIERREGOT - POOHEVILLERS - MARIEUX - SARTON.	
AMPLIERS		12.30pm	Arrived in billets at AMPLIERS.	
"	5.11.16	7.45am	Brigade marched to LIGNY-SUR-CANCHE via DOULLENS - BOUQUEMAISON - FREVENT	
LIGNY-SUR-CANCHE		3.15 pm	Arrived in billets at LIGNY-sur-CANCHE	
	6.11.16	6.30 am	The Brigade moved away from LIGNY-SUR-CANCHE and marched to FONTAINE-LEZ-BOULANS via NUNCQ - ST POL - ANVIN - BERGUENEUSE - HEUCHIN -	
FONTAINE		4.30pm	Arrived in billets at FONTAINE.	

Army Form C. 2118

WAR DIARY
INTELLIGENCE SUMMARY
(Erase heading not required.)

Instructions regarding War Diaries and Intelligence Summaries are contained in F. S. Regs., Part II. and the Staff Manual respectively. Title Pages will be prepared in manuscript.

Place	Date	Hour	Summary of Events and Information	Remarks and references to Appendices
FONTAINE LEZ BOULANS	7.11.16		Rested at FONTAINES.	
"	8.11.16		Rested at FONTAINE	
"	9.11.16	6.30 am	Brigade left FONTAINE and marched to GUARDBECQUE via WESTREHEM - ST HILAIRES - HAM-EN-ARTOIS - BERGUETTE.	
GUARDBECQE	12 noon		Arrived in billets at GAURDBECQUE	
GUARDBECQE	10.11.16	8.30 am	Brigade marched from GUARDBECQUE to STAPLE via ST YENANT - HAZEBROUCK - WALLON CAPPELL	
STAPLES		3.45 pm	Arrived at STAPLE in billets. Advanced parties consisting of O.C's and one other officer per battery went on ahead to start taking over from the Australians	
"	11.11.16	6.30 am	Brigade marched from STAPLE to BOESCHEPE via ST SYLVESTRE CAPPEL - EECKE - GODEWAERSVELDE.	
BOESCHEPE	"	12.30 pm	Arrived in billets at BOESCHEPE	
"	12.11.16		Rested at BOESCHEPE.	

Army Form C. 2118

WAR DIARY
INTELLIGENCE SUMMARY
(Erase heading not required.)

Instructions regarding War Diaries and Intelligence Summaries are contained in F.S. Regs., Part II. and the Staff Manual respectively. Title Pages will be prepared in manuscript.

Place	Date	Hour	Summary of Events and Information	Remarks and references to Appendices
BOESCHEPE	13.11.16		During the day the right sections of batteries relieved the right sections of 12 Bde A.F.A.	
near DICKEBUSCH	14.11.16		The remaining sections came up with H.Qs and the relief was completed. Lt Col C A GARDEN took over command of the DIEPENDAAL (right) GROUP consisting of the 190th Bde batteries as well as C/84 and D/184. Registration carried out during the day	
"	15.11.16		Registration continued. Capt. I.M. BROWNE RAMC killed and 1 O.R. wounded. Usual intermittent firing during the day otherwise nothing to report.	
	16.11.16		Nothing to report. H.A. D.A. 00 No 39 received, giving details of a raid on the enemy trenches round the HOLLANDSCHESSUR SALIENT on Nov 22nd.	
	17.11.16		Nothing to report	
	18.11.16		Nothing to report	
	19.11.16		Nothing to report	
	20.11.16		Nothing to report. O.O. 39 postponed. This operation was eventually postponed until the next month.	
	21.11.16		Preliminary orders for re-organisation received	
	22.11.16		Nothing to report.	

WAR DIARY
INTELLIGENCE SUMMARY

Army Form C. 2118

Place	Date	Hour	Summary of Events and Information	Remarks and references to Appendices
near DICKEBUSH	23.11.16		Re-organisation scheme received. The Brigade to consist of three 18th Batteries and one 6-gun Hows.	
	24.11.16		Nothing to report	
	25.11.16		Re-organisation commenced	
	26.11.16		Re-organisation completed. Composition of the Brigade as follows:- A/190 Consist of Hats B/163 and right section of old A/190, commanded by Capt. J. Erwald. M.C. RFA. B/190 commanded by Capt. N.H. Hutterbach consist of old B/190 and left section of old A/190. C/190 commanded by Major Spencer Smith (act) consist of old C/190 with right section of C/163. D/190 commanded by Capt. G.L. Leventhorpe consist of old D/163 and right section of old D/164. C/184 and B/184 went to the ST ELOI group.	Worcestre for OC 190 Bde RFA
	27.11.16		Nothing to report	
	28.11.16		Nothing to report	
	29.11.16		Nothing to report	
	30.11.16		Nothing to report	

WAR DIARY or INTELLIGENCE SUMMARY

Army Form C. 2118

190 Bde R.F.A. Vol 8

Place	Date	Hour	Summary of Events and Information	Remarks and references to Appendices
NEAR DICKEBUSCH	1-12-16		A quiet day. Registration for O.O. No 39½ completed by batteries	
"	2-12-16		Quiet Day.	
	3-12-16	12.35 / 12.47	Zero hour for the raid on HOLLANDSCHE=SCHUUR SALIENT (O.O. No 39½) A preliminary bombardment of 30 mins was carried out. 18 R. battery of the Group bombarded hostile F.L.T. and after Zero hour formed a box barrage round the salient. 4.5" Hows fired on the sunken roads in rear of the Salient. The raid was a success. Ammunition expended. Remember 7 th day ammunition 7 gunners	
	4-12-16		Quiet Day.	
	5-12-16		Armagh batteries were reorganised again into 4 gun batteries. Capt Kenaloffe's battery became A/169 (from D/190) and remains in the Group. Capt Vinets battery D/169 goes to ---- & Capt Jenkins becomes D/190, one section of his battery being in the Group, one sect. ST. ELOI front. Annie's Day.	
	6-12-16		Quiet day except for some hostile T.M. activity which was stopped by retaliation.	
	7-12-16		Nothing to report. Lt Col right ------ ----- --- was assumed the temp. ------- -- Col Cardew's absence on leave.	

WAR DIARY
or
INTELLIGENCE SUMMARY
(Erase heading not required.)

Army Form C. 2118

Instructions regarding War Diaries and Intelligence Summaries are contained in F.S. Regs., Part II. and the Staff Manual respectively. Title Pages will be prepared in manuscript.

Place	Date	Hour	Summary of Events and Information	Remarks and references to Appendices
NEAR BRIMESBATCN	8-12-16		Nothing to report.	
	9-12-16		Everything very quiet owing to continued bad weather. Capt J.B. MILNE proceeded to G.H.Q. via R. ADAMS.	
	10-12-16		Bad weather continues, hostile T.M. activity rather above normal. At 6 p.m. a short was carried out in conjunction with ST. ELOI Group on all works in enemy back country with aim to disturb traffic. All batteries employed.	
	11-12-16		Nothing to report.	
	12-12-16		Hostile T.M.'s again very active during the day on spot of Rumpelsdorn by D/89. D/90, D/90 & C/90.	
	13-12-16		None except hostile T.M. activity.	
	14-12-16		Quiet day. At about 6:50 p.m. enemy opened a heavy bombardment — chiefly with T.M.'s on our front line opposite Bois Quarante. Retaliation was fired by A/90, C/90 — (9 p.m. at 9.15 p.m.) C/90, D/90 received S.O.S. v A/90 at 9.30 p.m. The enemy attempted to raid our trenches but only our own fire was out and the attempt was a failure. Everything was quiet by 10.15 p.m.	
	15/12/16		Very quiet day.	

WAR DIARY or INTELLIGENCE SUMMARY

Army Form C. 2118

Place	Date	Hour	Summary of Events and Information	Remarks and references to Appendices
NEAR DICKEBUSCH	16.12.16		A bombardment of the enemy's front line system took place on the 47th Div. front. On the operations at Hours 7/189 accounted for 100 rds.	
	17.12.16		Very quiet day. Since the raid there has been very little activity on the part of the Bn. 7.1%	
	18.12.16		Very quiet, nothing to report.	
	19.12.16		Lt. Col. CARDEN returned from leave and resumed command of the Group again.	
	20.12.16		Very quiet all day.	
	21.12.16		Enemy shelled vicinity of CAPE BRIDGE during the morning, but considered retaliation by the Corps heavies + D/190 & 7/190. Nothing to report.	
	22.12.16			
	23.12.16		Enemy shelled the MEERSTRAAT ROAD continually during the morning Observation fair.	
	24.12.16		Observation very poor. Enemy Trench Mortars active on our front line from N.12.c.2.1 — N.13.d.6.6.	
	25.12.16		A bombardment of the enemy's new work for his operation at Hooge 7/189 firing 120 rounds, & 141 Trench mortar battery, & from 7/190 firing 100 rounds; & from C/190 firing 180 rounds in accordance with order P.M.O.6. N° 45.	

Army Form C. 2118

WAR DIARY
or
INTELLIGENCE SUMMARY
(Erase heading not required.)

Instructions regarding War Diaries and Intelligence Summaries are contained in F. S. Regs., Part II. and the Staff Manual respectively. Title Pages will be prepared in manuscript.

Place	Date	Hour	Summary of Events and Information	Remarks and references to Appendices
NEAR PICARDBUSCAT	26.12.16		Nothing to report.	
	27.12.16		In accordance with 41st D.A. O.O. No 47 B/190 fired 30 rds, 30 rds, observation fair, in conjunction with our T.M's. 1 section of D/190 fired 60 rounds in accordance with 168 Div Arty operation Order, nothing else to report. Observation very good, Enemy Trench Mortar retd all Batteries in the area & on hill T.M.S	
	29.12.16		Group retaliated and to good effect.	
	30.12.16		The following batteries fired in accordance with 41st A.A. O.O. No 46. 4 (Howr) D/189 fired 80rds, 6 June D/190 fired 30rds, 6 June Y/90 fired 90rds, 3 (Howr) B/190 fired 90 rds, 6 June B/190 fired 90rds. Mortars fired 40rds. Object of shoots to destroy Enemy T.M's. Enemy Trench Mortars active owing to our own artillery cutting our own wire by order of 41st Div. A.O.O. No 48. Nothing else to report.	
	31.12.16			

C.J. Javill Lt R.F.A
for Lt. Col. R.F.A.
O.o m.dg. 190th (Wimbledon) Bde. R.F.A.

WAR DIARY
or
INTELLIGENCE SUMMARY

(Erase heading not required.)

Army Form C. 2118

190 Bde R.F.A.

Place	Date	Hour	Summary of Events and Information	Remarks and references to Appendices
DICKE BUSCH	1.1.17		Quiet day.	
	2.1.17		A/190 position shelled with 10.5 c.m. for about 3 hours, casualties 1 O.R. wounded. A/190 O.P. shelled, 2/Lt. W. MUIR wounded and 1 O.R. killed.	
	3.1.17		Nothing to report. 2/Lieut A.E. KEATES posted to D/190.	
	4.1.17		Hostile artillery rather more active in rear of SCOTTISH WOOD – otherwise quiet.	
	5.1.17		Very quiet all day.	
	6.1.17		Hostile T.M's active during the morning. D/190 retaliated heavily.	
	7.1.17		A/190 shelled during with about 600 5.9" & 4.2" Hows. No casualties. C/190 commenced deliberate wire cutting about 03d 4.9 in accordance with 4th D.A. O. No.51, in preparation for a raid.	
	8.1.17		Quiet day. 4.5" How. batteries reorganised – the new D/190 being made up of A/189 (Capt. G. LEVENTHORPE) and one section of D/190(O.B) – commanded by Capt. G. LEVENTHORPE. The other section of the late D/190 became D/189.	

WAR DIARY
or
INTELLIGENCE SUMMARY

(Erase heading not required.)

Army Form C. 2118

Instructions regarding War Diaries and Intelligence Summaries are contained in F. S. Regs., Part II. and the Staff Manual respectively. Title Pages will be prepared in manuscript.

Place	Date	Hour	Summary of Events and Information	Remarks and references to Appendices
DICKEBUSCH	9.1.17		Nothing to report.	
LA CLYTTE	10.1.17		Brigade H.Q. Staff moved to new H.Q. at LA CLYTTE. Day very quiet. Hostile T.M.'s active during the afternoon, strong retaliation by D/190 and C/190 reduced them to silence.	
"	11.1.17		Nothing to report.	
	12.1.17		Divisional Group H.Q. 187 Bde. moved to LA CLYTTE and relieving the Bde. t assuming command of the DIEPENDAAL GROUP. A/190 & B/190 came out of the line to rest in their wagon lines. B/189 & C/189 taking their place in the line. Bde. H.Q. Staff moved back to DICKEBUSCH. C/190 & D/190 remained under command of DIEPENDAAL GROUP.	
	13.1.17		Nothing to report.	
	14.1.17		Nothing to report. O.C. Bde. inspects B/190 in marching order at their wagon lines.	
	15.1.17		Capt. S.A. FERRIER transferred to 187 Bde. to take command of A/187.	

WAR DIARY
or
INTELLIGENCE SUMMARY
(Erase heading not required.)

Army Form C. 2118

Instructions regarding War Diaries and Intelligence Summaries are contained in F. S. Regs, Part II. and the Staff Manual respectively. Title Pages will be prepared in manuscript.

Place	Date	Hour	Summary of Events and Information	Remarks and references to Appendices
	16.1.17.		Lt. Col. G.A. CARDEW D.S.O. temporarily took over command of 41st B.A. in place of Brig-Gen. S. Leverington C.B. C.M.G. Major N.H. Huttenbach M.C. took over command of Brigade.	
	17.1.17.			
	18.1.17.		Lt.Col. G.A. CARDEW inspects A/190 in marching order. Their wagon lines. Line entertained by 123rd Bde. in St Eloi Sector. C/190 arrives in barrage to D/190 in bombardment.	
	19.1.17.		Nothing to report.	
	20.1.17.		C/190 comes out of the line being relieved by 34th Battery R.F.A. & D/190 by D/169 Bde & came back to their wagon lines to rest.	
	21.1.17.		Major L.W. SAVILLE D.S.O. took over command the Brigade vice Major N.H. HUTTENBACH M.C. D.S.O. Nothing to report.	
	22.1.17.		Brigade marches back to RYVELD billets for a period of rest & training.	

WAR DIARY
or
INTELLIGENCE SUMMARY

(Erase heading not required.)

Army Form

Place	Date	Hour	Summary of Events and Information	Remarks and references to Appendices
RYVELD	24.1.17 to 31.1.17		Brigade remained at RYVELD resting. During the whole period it froze hard, day and night and training was confined to walks as it was impossible to get vehicles or horses on the roads. On Jan 26th the O.C. Bn. & Adjutant went up to reconnoitre positions in the Salient (in 23rd Div. area) in front of YPRES as a precautionary measure in case the Brigade was called upon to go up in reserve. A working party of 76 was sent up to work on these positions.	

JM Spencer-Smith
Major RFA
Comdg. 180th (Wimbledon) Bde. RFA

WAR DIARY or INTELLIGENCE SUMMARY

Army Form C. 2118

190 BM R20 Vol 10

Place	Date	Hour	Summary of Events and Information	Remarks and references to Appendices
RYVELD	1.2.17		2/Lieut. P.S. Preston R.g.a. struck off Strength of A/190 & posted attached to C/190.	
"	2.2.17		Nothing to report. Owing to continued hard frost, training was practically out of the question	
"	3.2.17			
"	4.2.17			
"	5.2.17			
"	6.2.17			
"	7.2.17		2/Lieut. A.P. CUNDALL posted to A/190 2/Lieut. E.W. HORNCASTLE " B/190 } as reinforcements. Following Officers posted 6.4.15. 2/Lieut. J.C. FERGUSSON " D/190 D.A.C. 2/Lieut A.G. HARPER from D/190 & 2/Lieut. H.S. FRENCH from A/190	
"	8.2.17		Nothing to report.	
"	9.2.17			
"	10.2.17			
"	11.2.17			

Army Form C. 2118

WAR DIARY
or
INTELLIGENCE SUMMARY
(Erase heading not required.)

Instructions regarding War Diaries and Intelligence Summaries are contained in F.S. Regs., Part II. and the Staff Manual respectively. Title Pages will be prepared in manuscript.

Place	Date	Hour	Summary of Events and Information	Remarks and references to Appendices
RYVELD	12.2.17		Major-Gen. FRANKS, M.G.R.A. 2nd Army inspected B/190 with a view to sending them to the 2nd. Army Artillery School. Major L.W. SAVILE left to take over command of 25th Bde. Army F.A. in the 1st Army Area. Major G.M. SPENCER SMITH took over temporary command of the Brigade. One Section per battery moved out to go up to the line and take over from the 189th Bde. in the DIEPENDAAL GROUP.	
	13.2.17		Nothing to report.	
LA CLYTTE	14.2.17		Remaining two sections per battery of Bde. Headquarters moved up to DIEPENDAAL GROUP and took over from 189 Bde.	
	15.2.17	6.30 a.m.	Group Shoot on IN DEN STERKE CABT and GOUDEZEUNE FARM (015A32 & 015L7.4, Sheet 28 S.W.) D/190 combated the buildings & 18 Pr. battery barraged. Ammunition expended Q16AX & 125 BX.	

WAR DIARY
or
INTELLIGENCE SUMMARY
(Erase heading not required.)

Army Form C. 2118

Instructions regarding War Diaries and Intelligence Summaries are contained in F.S. Regs., Part II. and the Staff Manual respectively. Title Pages will be prepared in manuscript.

Place	Date	Hour	Summary of Events and Information	Remarks and references to Appendices
LA CLYTTE	16.2.17		Some T. Hostile T.M. activity during the afternoon, but D/190 and C/190 retaliated heavily and this soon ceased. Lieut. H. DOBBINSON, R.F.A. posted to D/190 from T.M.'s. M.C.	
	17.2.17		A quiet day until about 4.15 p.m. when the enemy opened a heavy bombardment on our front & support lines in the neighbourhood of BOIS CARRÉ. This continued until about 6 p.m. when everything quietened down. No infantry action followed. All batteries retaliated heavily so as to hold F.L.T and BOIS QUARANTE. The Group fired about 500 rds.	
	18.2.17		Quiet day except for some hostile shelling of our trenches which was stopped by prompt retaliation from A/190.	
	19.2.17		Some hostile trench mortar activity about the centre of the Group front at 2.50 p.m. this caused upon retaliation from D/190 & A/190.	
	20.2.17	5 p.m.	Raid carried out by 47th Div. on our left. D/190 assisted by bombarding WHITE CHATEAU (O4d.1.7). Raid very successful, over 100 prisoners taken.	

2/Lieut L.W.M. TAYLOR posted A/190 from 4th D.A.C.

WAR DIARY
or
INTELLIGENCE SUMMARY

(Erase heading not required.)

Army Form C. 2118

Instructions regarding War Diaries and Intelligence Summaries are contained in F.S. Regs., Part II. and the Staff Manual respectively. Title Pages will be prepared in manuscript.

Place	Date	Hour	Summary of Events and Information	Remarks and references to Appendices
EA CUTTE	21.2.17		Quiet morning. During the afternoon there was some intermittent shelling of our trenches with 7.7cms. & M.T.M.'s this was promptly answered by batteries of the Group & ceased after 3.30p.m. The four batteries of 187th Bde. came up to the Group as coufacing batteries for a daylight raid to take place on the HOLLAND SCHEISCHR & SALIENT. Owing to foggy weather, registration was impossible.	
	22.2.17		X Day — 8 previous bombardment took place with 2gw. owing to conditions foggy. Some registration was possible for the 187 Bdes. however.	
	23.2.17		X Day bombardment took place and Y day was cancelled altogether. Digo bombardee area to be raided and 187's Scocles troops with one 187 Bary. did not fire. This was done in conjunction with Heavy Artillery. Ammunition expended 350A, 500Ax, 1200 Bx.	
	24.2.17	4.55pm	Z day — bombardment by hour, during the morning. Zero hour. 187th batteries from former peak of the creeping barrage	

WAR DIARY
or
INTELLIGENCE SUMMARY

(Erase heading not required.)

Army Form C. 2118

Place	Date	Hour	Summary of Events and Information	Remarks and references to Appendices
LA CLYTTE	24.2.17	4.5 Hours	Lombards French in rear. 185th battery joined in the standing barrage when they reached it, with the exception of C/190 who were at disposal. All guns again at 6.30 p.m. Raid very successful & over 50 prisoners captured. See attached report. Ammunition expended — 800A 1625AA, 1150RX.	
	25.2.16		Very quiet day, nothing to report.	
	26.2.16		One Section of 34th Batty. relieved B/190.	
	27.2.16		Remainder of 34th Batty relieved B/190, & the latter marched back to 2nd Army Artillery School.	
	28.2.16		Nothing to report.	

R. L. Smart
MAJOR R.F.A.

SECRET.   REPORT OF RAID ON THE HOLLANDSCHESHURR REDOUBT

All arrangements in connection with the Raid were made personnally with the Brigade Major 124th Infantry and the Observation Post selected in COCKATOO TRENCH was occupied at 3 p.m. this afternoon.

Up to about 4.20 p.m. everything was abnormally quiet on the whole front that could be seen, but at about this time the Germans put a certain amount of T.M. shells, 4.2" and 5.9" shells into our trenches near CHICORY LANE this continued at only a fair rate until our bombardment commenced. It was particularly noticeable that NO shells of any sort were put on the area odcupied by the party who were doing the Raid.

Our bombardment and barrage started percisely at the times laid down, and although the visibility waspoor it was noticed that the shrapnel appeared to burst well, with the exception of a few shells on the right.   At about 5.1 p.m. Captain Bray (ourR.A. Liaison Officer) asked for the creeping barrage tomlift, and this message was immediately forwarded to H.Q. DIEPENDAAL GROUP, and no further message with regard to the Barrage was received.

At about 5.15 p.m. a message was received from Captain Bray that our Raiding party had passed safely over and captured about 30 prisoners. Our guns seemed to keep up a good rate of fire, and the only reply from the Germans Guns was on our front line and on WATLING STREET (16th Div Area) the latter being heavily shelled throughout the operation.

From time to time messages were received from Captain Bray, as f far as the telephone lines permitted, they were as under:-

5.10 p.m. 1 gun of creeping barrage shooting short – rectified.
5.20 p.m. Quicken up standing barrage and search and sweep – Batteries concerned were informed.
5.25 p.m. Front Line Trench and WATLING STREET heavily shelled.– Xth Corps Counter Batteries informed.
5.46 p.m. Machine Gun at O.7.c,3½.4. reported active –
1 Howitzer Gun D/190 and 2 Guns C/190 turned on to this and ST ELOI GROUP informed.

At 5.55 p.m. the signal to withdraw was sent up, and at 6 p.m. a message was received asking for the rate of fire to be quickened up for 15 minutes during the withdrawal, the result of this message was very pronounced.

At 6.24 p.m. having received a message that the withdrawal was practically completed, I ordered fire to be slackened by half, and at 6.30 p.m. cease fire was sent round to Batteries.

All was quiet for a while but at about 6.45 p.m. a few shell fell near POPPY LANE Communication Trench.

24-2-1917.

WAR DIARY or INTELLIGENCE SUMMARY

Army Form C. 2118

190th Bde R.F.A.

Place	Date	Hour	Summary of Events and Information	Remarks and references to Appendices
La Clytte	1.3.17		2Lt. L. Humphreys RFA & 2Lt E.W Horncastle RFA transferred to A/190 from B/190 when the latter marched out to 2nd Army Artillery School Tilques. 2Lt. W.A. Mackenzie RFA joined Headquarters of the Brigade with a view to taking over duties of Adjutant in the near future. Nothing to report.	
	2.3.17		Nothing to report.	
	3.3.17		Orders received for "P.B." Shoot to be carried out on the 7th inst	
	4.3.17	12.30 PM	Dufendaal Group O.O. NO. 11 Scheme "A" took place at 12.30PM in which 4 Howitzers D/190 bombarded Dugouts at 0.13.a.25.55. & the 34th Bty RFA placed a Box Barrage round this point for 4 minutes. Total Ammunition 15 rds A 35 rds A.X. 40 rds B.X. Schemes "B" "C" "D" & "E" were cancelled by Division owing to shortage of Ammunition available	
	5.3.17		Nothing to report.	
	6.3.17			
	7.3.17	6.30 am	"P.B. Shoot" – Barrage along line 07.c.7.8½ – 07.d.0.0½ in lifts of 50 yds to 07.d.1½.7 – 07.d.0.6 4 rds per gun per minute for 5 minutes = 360 rds A.X. 2Lt. R.G. Russell joined the Brigade from Hospital & posted to A/190.	

Army Form C. 2118

WAR DIARY

INTELLIGENCE SUMMARY

190th Bde R.F.A.

(Erase heading not required.)

Instructions regarding War Diaries and Intelligence Summaries are contained in F.S. Regs., Part II. and the Staff Manual respectively. Title Pages will be prepared in manuscript.

Place	Date	Hour	Summary of Events and Information	Remarks and references to Appendices
La Clytte	8.3.17		Nothing to report.	
	9.3.17			
	10.3.17			
	11.3.17		Captain J. C. O'Callaghan R.F.A. Cmdg C/190th Bde R.F.A. appointed A/Major (Subsequently antedated to 14.2.17.) 2.Lt. A.G. Harper transferred from Trench Mortars to A/190 Bde R.F.A.	
	12.3.17		Nothing to report.	
	13.3.17			
	14.3.17		Major N.H. Huttenbach R.F.A. awarded the "Silver medal for military Valour" by the Italian Government.	
	15.3.17		Nothing to report.	
	16.3.17			
	17.3.17		Lt. C.F Farrill R.F.A. promoted A/Captain & posted as second-in-Command of C/190. Lt. W.A. Mackenzie A/190 appointed Adjutant of the Brigade (Both these appointments subsequently antedated to 14.2.17.)	

1875 Wt. W593/826 1,000,000 4/15 J.B.C. & A. A.D.S.S./Forms/C. 2118.

Army Form C. 2118

WAR DIARY
INTELLIGENCE SUMMARY
(Erase heading not required.)

190th Bde RFA

Place	Date	Hour	Summary of Events and Information	Remarks and references to Appendices
La Clytte	17.3.17		2/Lt. R. Heaton R.F.A. transferred from A/190 to B/187. All 18 Pr. Batteries fired 6 rds per Battery on communications during the night turned the "G.E." Shoot (Good evening) & they also fired 24 rds each on working parties between 40' before Sunrise to 40' after Sunrise termed the "G.M." Shoot (Good Morning)	
	18.3.17		The two operations named above were repeated on this day. Ammunition allotment was this day reduced to 100 rds A.X. per Group & 12 rds B.X. Major N.H. Huttenbach being posted to England as a Gunnery Instructor was struck off the strength of this Brigade. T/Captain & T. Dorrell R.F.A. posted to command B/190 in his place. 2/Lt. E.W. Horncastle R.F.A. transferred from A/190 to C/190.	
	19.3.17	6.10am	In conjunction with Stokes Mortars & Machine Guns of 124th Inf. Bde a Batteries carried out a combined shoot on German Working Parties behind	
		6.40am		

Army Form C. 2118.

WAR DIARY
INTELLIGENCE SUMMARY
(Erase heading not required.)

190th Bde R.F.A.

Place	Date	Hour	Summary of Events and Information	Remarks and references to Appendices
La Clytte	19.3.17		(Contd) the HOLLANDSCHESCHUUR SALIENT - the 18 Prs. firing on trench from N.8.6.9. - N.8.6.75.90 & from PLATEAU FARM to N.1.8.5¼.6½ while the 4.5 Hows silenced the enemy M.T.M's in this district. Total ammunition 200 rds A.X. 100 rds B.X. Result - very good indeed, among the debris thrown up were seen shovels & building material.	
	20.3.17		Major P. Shefford D.S.O. R.F.A attached to Head quarters 190th Bde R.F.A.	
	21.3.17		2.Lt. A.G. Harper R.F.A. posted to Trench Mortars from A/190. 2.Lt. E.W. Horncastle R.F.A. do do do C/190.	
	22.3.17		One Section of each Battery relieved on this evening by a Section of Batteries of the 180th Bde R.F.A. 16th Division. Major P. Shefford D.S.O. R.F.A left the Brigade to be attached to 187 Bde R.F.A.	
	23.3.17		Remainder of Brigade relieved by 180th Bde - On Completion of relief Batteries returned to their wagon lines & Headquarters to farm at N.1.a.3.2.	

Army Form C. 2118

WAR DIARY
INTELLIGENCE SUMMARY
(Erase heading not required.)

190th Bde R.F.A.

Instructions regarding War Diaries and Intelligence Summaries are contained in F. S. Regs., Part II. and the Staff Manual respectively. Title Pages will be prepared in manuscript.

Place	Date	Hour	Summary of Events and Information	Remarks and references to Appendices
Sheet 28 N1a 3.2.	24.3.17		Batteries warned to start building gun pits in front of Dickebusch Lake about H.35.a & b early following morning.	
	25.3.17		Batteries start work on Wagon lines while all available men & horses. 1 Officer & 40 men per Battery start digging gun positions. G.O.C. 41st Division inspects the horses of the Brigade	require more accommodation mentioned above
	26.3.17		Nothing to report - weather very windy & wet.	
	27.3.17			
	28.3.17			
	29.3.17		Batteries continue to build gun Positions weather, very stormy & wet.	
	30.3.17			
	31.3.17			

E.A. Gardner Lt. Col. R.F.A.
Commanding 190th Bde R.F.A.

WAR DIARY

INTELLIGENCE SUMMARY

Army Form C. 2118

190th Bde R.F.A.

JC 12

Place	Date	Hour	Summary of Events and Information	Remarks and references to Appendices
Sheet 28 N 1a 3 2	1.4.17		Batteries continue to dig new positions on slope between RIDGE WOOD & SCOTTISH WOOD.	
	2.4.17		On April 2nd while going to work 2 men of C/190 were killed & one wounded. Col Cowden took over command of ⚡ELOI Group on cal Swords proceeding to England on leave	
	3.4.17		Batteries take up ammunition to positions they will occupy following night to assist in raid by 47th Division on our left.	
	4.4.17		Batteries take guns up into positions in St ELOI Section	
	5.4.17			
	6.4.17		Batteries registered for shoot on the 7th inst.	
	7.4.17		Raid at 8 P.M. by 47th Divn North of Canal. Batteries of the Brigade assist with Dummy Barrage on S.ELOI Craters about 07c & 07d from 7.50 P.M. to 8.10 P.M. See Hist DA. O.O. NO. 64 & 47th DA. O.O. NO. 21. Enemy shell our very slight round our Batteries. We fire our guns out of action after 12 midnight, withdraw to wagon lines. Col Cowden handed over command of S.ELOI Group to Major Harford 187 Bde R.F.A. returned to 190th H.Q. N1a 32.	
	8.4.17		Brigade prepared to march out to S.OMER training area in the morning	

1875 Wt. W593/826 1,000,000 4/15 J.B.C. & A. A.D.S.S./Forms/C. 2118.

WAR DIARY

Army Form C. 2118

INTELLIGENCE SUMMARY

190th Bde R.F.A.

(Erase heading not required.)

Instructions regarding War Diaries and Intelligence Summaries are contained in F.S. Regs., Part II. and the Staff Manual respectively. Title Pages will be prepared in manuscript.

Place	Date	Hour	Summary of Events and Information	Remarks and references to Appendices
N 1 a 3 2	9.4.17		Brigade marched out to NOORDPEENE via Cassel — leaving Renninghelst church at 9.30 a.m. to 10.30 am arriving between 5 & 6 P.M. — weather very stormy — billets very satisfactory — passed 189th Bde RFA at STEENVOORDE — marching in to occupy our wagon lines.	
	10.4.17		Inspected by G.O.C. 41st Div. at 9 a.m. Went Brigade proceeds to MUNCQ-NIEURLET via WATTEN — arriving about 2.30 P.M. weather very bad. Col Carden adjutant called on 123rd Bde at GANSPETTE on the way.	
	11.4.17		Brigade Battery Staffs parade in Area X — short shower — weather very bad — afternoon — gundrill stables.	
	12.4.17		Training under Battery arrangements — Dummy drill & skeleton Drill Order — weather very bad again — groung very heavy for horses — Colonel Carden & adjutant met General Gordon 123rd Bde — discussed combined work for following week	
	13.4.17		Visit of G.O.C. 41st Division who inspected batteries training on the training area, weather cold but fine.	

Army Form C. 2118

WAR DIARY
INTELLIGENCE SUMMARY

190th Bde R.F.A

(Erase heading not required.)

Place	Date	Hour	Summary of Events and Information	Remarks and references to Appendices
MUNCQ - NIEURLET South of AUDRUICQ	14.4.17		Horses left in Billets to rest after the heavy work on the day before. Batteries had Gun drill & lectures in billets.	
	15.4.17		Sunday. Half-holiday ordered for Brigade. Weather very bad all day - strong wind & rain incessantly.	
	16.4.17		Brigade practised an Advance Guard attack - most instructive.	
	17.4.17		Work under Battery arrangements, very stormy weather.	
	18.4.17		do. G.O.C. R.A. 41st Divn. arrived about 10 a.m. & inspected each Battery in Stables returning to RENINGHELST after lunch.	
	19.4.17		Practice attack from Trench Warfare with the 123rd Inf. Bde. Batteries occupied positions for Barrage fire. G.O.C. 41st Divn. witnessed the attack. Weather bad.	
	20.4.17		Repetition of previous day's attack witnessed by Army Commander. Batteries returned & occupied fresh positions.	

Army Form C. 2118.

WAR DIARY
INTELLIGENCE SUMMARY.
(Erase heading not required.)

190th Bde R.F.A.

Place	Date	Hour	Summary of Events and Information	Remarks and references to Appendices
MUNCQ NIEVLET	21.4.17		Attack from Trench Warfare repeated before Xth Corps Commander. Batteries advanced to a second position & were inspected in action by G.O.C. 10th Corps & G.O.C. 41st Division. - Drill training throughout was excellent, perfect communication was maintained throughout the attack from Batteries to Brigade & from F.O.O.'s with the Infantry and Brigade. Weather bright fine, ground was a bit dry under a N.E. wind which made the going easier for the horses. 2/Lt B.C. Metge from D.A.C. to D/190	
	22.4.17		Rest for men & horses prior to marching back to Renninghelst area the following day. Results of training. Drill throughout greatly improved - all ranks smartened up after a long period of Trench Warfare - horses condition considerably improved & hardened by the hard work though by no means fat owing to short forage rations.	
	23.4.17		Start of the march back to Divisional Area. In conjunction with the 123rd Inf Bde we marched as an Advance guard. A/190 formed part of the Vanguard starting from WATTEN at 8.5 a.m. - remainder of Brigade	

WAR DIARY

INTELLIGENCE SUMMARY.

190th Bde R.F.A.

Army Form C. 2118.

Place	Date	Hour	Summary of Events and Information	Remarks and references to Appendices
MUNCQ NIEURLET	23.4.17	(contd)	passed the same place at 8.30 a.m. Arrival at OEHTEZEELE about 1 P.M. where we found excellent billets.	
OEHTEZEELE Sheet 28 N1a 32.	24.4.17		marched from here at 8 a.m. through CASSEL - A BEILE & RENINGHELST to wagon lines, arriving between 2 P.M. & 3 P.M. weather for the two days march was good - men & horses were the worse.	
	25.4.17		Nothing to report. Capt. G.H. Oakes from D.T.M.O. to D/190. 2/Lt H. Parker 6/1/90 to Trench	2/Lt H. Parker 6/1/90 to Trench Mortars
	26.4.17		Battries sent up working parties of 1 Officer & 40 O.R.'s to dig new positions on slope between RIDGE WOOD & SCOTTISH WOOD.	Hills D/190
	27.4.17		} Nothing to report.	
	28.4.17			
	29.4.17			
	30.4.17		2/Lt G.D. Dale joined from Reinforcements - posted to D/190.	

Commdg 190 Bde R.F.A

Army Form C. 2118.

WAR DIARY
or
INTELLIGENCE SUMMARY
(Erase heading not required.)

190th Bde RFA.

WO 95/3118/3

Place	Date	Hour	Summary of Events and Information	Remarks and references to Appendices
Sheet 28 N1a 3.2	1.5.17		2/Lt. L. Hills A/190, & 2/Lt. H. Parker C/190 attached to Trench Mortars. 2/Lt S.C. Metge H/190 D.A.C. attached to D/190. 2/Lt. B. D. Dale attached to D/190 from Reinforcements.	
	2.5.17		Nothing to report.	
	3.5.17		2/Lt. H. E. Hockie attached to C/190 from Reinforcements. This Brigade started to relieve 187th Bde RFA. in the St. ELOI Sector, 3 guns of each Battery going up on this night A/190 relieving A/187, C/190 relieving B/187 & D/190 relieving D/187.	
	4.5.17		Relief of Headquarters 187th Bde by Headquarters 190th Bde complete by 8 am. do Batteries complete by 11.30 P.M.	
	5.5.17		Quiet day - weather fine - enemy shelled DICKEBUSCH Rd from that village to Café BELGE from 9PM to 10PM. from 10.15PM to 10.45 PM again from 11.15 PM to midnight & 1am to 1.30 am. The first round (10.5 cm) hit house at H.28.d.1.2. headquarters of N0 3 Belgian Battery, killing 3 men wounding 3 more.	
	6.5.17		Enemy shelled VOORMEZEELE - SNIPERS BARN (O.1.C.3.5) in the morning	

WAR DIARY
INTELLIGENCE SUMMARY.
(Erase heading not required.)

Army Form C. 2118.

190th Bde RFA

Place	Date	Hour	Summary of Events and Information	Remarks and references to Appendices
S E L 01 H.2. H28 & 7.8	6.5.17		In the afternoon Chateau SEGARD – Durnt at H 30 a 2.9. Stock areas enemy aeroplane directing most of the fire which consisted of 15 cms & 10.5cms Hows.	
			Just before 9 P.M. enemy started shelling the DICKEBUSCH Road from Cafe Belge to La Clytte village with 15cms & 10.5cms Hows. doing some damage to transport, then continued intermittently until 12 midnight. At 5.30 am enemy started shelling horse lines A/190 position at H29 b.3.1 with 15cms hows. an aeroplane directing the fire, no damage to materiel – Battn Sergt. Major T/Bdr. wounded in the leg. Enemy shelling of our Bdr areas most vigorous all the morning – unusually heavy all day.	
	7.5.17		2/Lt. Q.M. Harris A/190 attached to Trench Mortars. 2/Lt. E.W. Hornicastle attached to A/190 from Trench Mortars. Ammunition taken up from the 5th unit every night to new X Scheme positions in the St. Eloi Sector by Batteries & D.A.C. of this Division. Weather very hot today.	

WAR DIARY
INTELLIGENCE SUMMARY

Army Form C. 2118.

190th Bde. R.F.A.

Place	Date	Hour	Summary of Events and Information	Remarks and references to Appendices
S. ELOI Gp Headquarters	8.5.17		Party of 7 Officers & 153 O.R.s of 65th A.F.A. Bde arrived & were attached to Headquarters Batteries for instruction.	
			D/190 fired 40 rds for Counter Battery work on 0.17.a.2.8. & three retaliated for Trench Mortar firing on F.L.T.	
			18 Prs checked registration during the day.	
			Enemy appeared to be registering on VOORMEZEELE - the Batteries had a quiet day - weather very hot indeed.	
			Ammunition taken up each night to X Scheme positions.	
	9.5.17		At 6 am the enemy started shelling A/190's position with 5.9s & 4.2s from several directions - the first shell landed in a horse lined of a billet killing 2 O.R.s & wounding 2 O.R.s, one of the latter has since died of wounds. At about 8 am Bde hqrs 4/1 D.A. Lt. S. Phillips a.S.C. R.A. went round Battery Positions taken near A/190 (H.29.b) a shell burst wounding Mr Phillips in the leg & slightly wounding the Bde hqr. Shelling of the area continued intermittently all day long, special attention being paid in the afternoon to Heavy Battery positions behind this Headquarters.	
		10.30 a.m.	D/190 retaliated on Hostile Trench Mortar for shelling our	

Army Form C. 2118.

WAR DIARY
~~INTELLIGENCE~~ SUMMARY.
(Erase heading not required.)

190th Bde RFA

Place	Date	Hour	Summary of Events and Information	Remarks and references to Appendices
Sel oi Gard Halfnaste	9.5.17		Trenches opposite SELOI Crater and again about 1.30 PM at 8.45 PM all Batteries carried on 41st D.A. O.O. NO. 71 in a concentrated shoot of 15 minutes on German back areas — the 18 pr. Batteries the Belgians fired on the road running from SELOI village to BONDULLE FARM from about 08D75.90 to 015a 7.0. The tramway running on the DAMMSTRASSE at 0ga 82½ to 015a 4.0. D/190 concentrated on important trench road junctions in the same area. This Operation was repeated at 11.15 PM. Total ammunition 393 A9AX & 90 BK.	
	10.5.17		Enemy shelling confined to Back areas, VOORMEZEELE, Chateau SEGARD. D/190 fired 50 rds at 2 PM. on 017&4.6 & 017&2.8 for Counter Batteries 2nd Lt. H.E. McKie attached C/190 to Acting ADC RA. 41st Div¹ Arty 2nd Lt. I.H. Phillips 187th Bde RFA attached C/190. Ammunition brought up every night to X Scheme positions 1 Section A/190 moves to B1 position H35c 65.90	

WAR DIARY or **INTELLIGENCE SUMMARY.**

Army Form C. 2118.

190th Bde R.F.A.

Place	Date	Hour	Summary of Events and Information	Remarks
St Elor' group H.Q.	11.5.17		D/190 proceeded to England direct from T.I.g. up. Major Donnell V.C. having proceeded to Camp 26 from 2nd Army Arty School is struck off the strength. 2/Lt H Parker C/190 posted for Trench Mortars. 2/Lt L Hills D/190 do do. Our fire – nothing beyond registration. Enemy Fire – Café Belge 6.50 am 7 gun – no damage to Battery positions – Voormezeele + Back areas. Ammunition taken up so usual to X scheme positions. 1 Section A/190 moved to B1 position H 35 c 65.90.	
	12.5.17		Group Shoot on Dugouts about Og a 2 B 9 vicinity – D/190 bombarded these points for 5 minutes at 5 am – A/190 & C/190 formed a Box Barrage round them also for 5 minutes to catch runners. Ammunition 120 rds AK. 30 rds BX. Enemy Shelling:- 6.30 am to 10 am A/190 position at H 29 b was heavily shelled with 15 cm & How & 10.5 cm How. 2 guns hit only one of which out of action – telephone pit hit & equipment damaged, no casualties, 200 rds ammunition damaged.	

WAR DIARY
INTELLIGENCE SUMMARY.

Army Form C. 2118.

190th Bde R.F.A.

Place	Date	Hour	Summary of Events and Information	Remarks and references to Appendices
St Eloi Group Headquarters	12.5.17.		In addition to this the usual areas were shelled viz. VOORMEZEELE, Chateau SEGARD, Brick areas. Ammunition taken up as usual.	
	13.5.17.		3 Officers & 70 O.R.'s 65th A.F.A. Bde (504th Battery) returned to their Unit to-day.	
			D/190 fired 70 rds Counter Battery work at 2 P.M. M.T.M.'s of this Division cut wire at 1.30 P.M. in front of trenches F.L.T. from 08a.3.6 to 02d.10.65 & 02d.10.65 to 03c.7.5. Covered by this group who fired 90 AX & 40 BX. + 80 rounds.	
			C/190 were shelled by H.V. gun from N. of YPRES at very long range, no damage. Intermittent shelling from 7am to 11am. No ammunition was taken up in the day.	
	14.5.17.		C/190 (H30a) were shelled from 8am to 2 P.M. with 15 cms. 10.5 cms 77.7 cms from 12 noon to 2 P.M. with 21 cms. Mortars. A new piercing shell — enemy shelling in back areas in the afternoon.	

Army Form C. 2118.

WAR DIARY
—or—
INTELLIGENCE SUMMARY.
(Erase heading not required.)

190th Bde R.F.A.

Instructions regarding War Diaries and Intelligence Summaries are contained in F. S. Regs., Part II. and the Staff Manual respectively. Title pages will be prepared in manuscript.

Place	Date	Hour	Summary of Events and Information	Remarks and references to Appendices
St. Eloi	14.6.17		D/190 registered HIELE Fm. at 11.15 58 rds BX.	
H.2.		2 PM to 4 PM	A/190 cut wire from O3c 0.3½ to O3c 8½ 5. C/190 do do O2c 42.10 to D7b 9½ 3½	
		2 PM	D/190 fired 250 rds on enemy T.M. emplacements, O.P.s etc, in accordance with instructions received for 415 D.A.	
		4 PM		
		5:45	D/190 shot with 'Klune on Counter Battery target not very successful	
		8 PM	M T M's cut wire from O2ck.1 to O2c 6.3 & O2d 57. O3c 0.4. 177 Bombs in all	
			This Brigade covered the advance with 150rds AY 150 rds BX. E/190 from dusk to twilight fired 200 rds A on new trench O3d 75.20 – O3d 45.10 – O3d 35 60 – O3d 00.75. – O9a 85.65. 1 Section C/190 moved to E 4 horton at 1st & 30.55. 3 guns B/190 relieved No.1 Belgian Battery at N4b 85.75. 3 guns 504th Battery relieved No.2 do do at H34 C 1.5 1 Section No 3 Belgian Battery withdrawn from H34 d 10.65.	

Army Form C. 2118.

WAR DIARY
INTELLIGENCE SUMMARY

(Erase heading not required.)

190th Bde RFA.

Place	Date	Hour	Summary of Events and Information	Remarks and references to Appendices
St Eloi Sgt H.Q.	14.5.17		Ammunition came up by train in the night.	
	15.5.17		B/190 registered on front of left sector to reinforce A/190 South Bty do do do C/190 Right do do Hostile Artillery fairly quiet. Second Section C/190 moved up at night from H30a.15.65 to I 31.b 30.55. C/190 carried out night firing in conjunction with 1 Section D/190 on tracks in O9c & from O9d 7.8 to O9d 30.45. = 200 rds A1AK + 50 rds BX.	
	16.5.17		Hostile Artillery active in CAFÉ BELGE flank areas. 2 Lt Findley B/190 proceeded to 3days Course at ABEILE on ranging in open warfare. Wire has now been cut on right Sector of Divisional front, 9 from the Craters to RUINED FARM is considerably knocked about & benched. Nightfiring B/190 & 2 hows D/190 O 8 d 88.53. 9 trenches from O9C 30.35 - to O9c 50.35 & O8d 45.25 to O8d 63.30 & O9d 70.80 to O9c 40.10 200 rds A9AX & 50 BX.	
	17.5.17		2 Lt A.K. Andrews arrived from Reinforcements attached A/190.	

Army Form C. 2118

WAR DIARY
or
INTELLIGENCE SUMMARY
(Erase heading not required.)

190th Bde RFA

Place	Date	Hour	Summary of Events and Information	Remarks and references to Appendices
SE10 Headquarters	17.5.17		Hostile artillery active on VOORMEZEELE & Support Trenches. Night firing on O8a 70.73. O8a 15.60. O9a 75.36. O2d 35.50. O9c 80.48 to O9c 40 Dugouts & Tramway by 504th Bty. +2 Hour ammunition the same each night. 200 rds AJAX 50 rds BX. Silent raid at night by 20th Batt. D.L.I. in trenches O2e 3± O. This group stood by to render assistance by placing a Barrage round the point but were not called upon. Wire cutting took place as usual today – from O3c 40.28 to O3c 70.50 considerable damage by 18 Pr.	
	18.5.17		VOORMEZEELE track areas shelled intermittently throughout the day. This group stood by again for raid as for the 17th but were not called on to fire. Night targets were O10a 22.98 O10a 77.58 O10a 93.14. O10a 38.3.18 O10c 44.20 C/190 D/190 92 Hours.	
	19.5.17		VOORMEZEELE Support trenches & track areas shelled at e.g. D gale D/190 proceeded to X Corps Course for 3 days instruction in when weather permitting	

Army Form C. 2118.

WAR DIARY
or
INTELLIGENCE SUMMARY.
(Erase heading not required.)

190th Bde RFA

Place	Date	Hour	Summary of Events and Information	Remarks and references to Appendices
Steeni H2	19.5.17		Section of C/190 moved from H29c 60.75 to I31.6 30.55. at night to do H35c 65 90 to H35c 40.30. A/190	
			Ammunition continues to be brought up by train each night to X Scheme position under Lt. Col. G. Symonds 187th Bde RFA.	
			Night targets O3d 45 57 & O3d 35 43 & D10a 22 98 Trench Junctions	
			O8d 90 78, O8d 88 86 O8d 80.90 Strong Points	
			O10a 70.58 Dugouts A/190 72 Hows.	
	20.5.17		VOORMEZEELE, CHATEAU SEGARD &ck area shelled during the day B/190 (N4 & 85, 79) & G. van Farm shelled at noon with 250 15cm How. H.V. gun (10 cm) from North of YPRES shelled new position E of DICKEBUSCH Lake - fires up about 350 rds. 18 Pr. am. at H35c 40.30. B/190 suffered no damage beyond Telephone & Officers Dugouts destroyed.	
		5am	4 How D/190 harassed Dugouts at 09 a 2. 8. South & B/190 ferred	
			Box Barrage and it - Operation lasted 5 minutes A9 a X 120 BX 3b.	
		6.20 PM	4 How D/190 fired on dump at O10 6 22. C/190 fired bursts of fire at 6.20 & 7 PM on same point 120 ds BX, 32 rds AX	

Army Form C. 2118.

WAR DIARY
or
INTELLIGENCE SUMMARY.
(Erase heading not required.)

190th Bde R.F.A.

Place	Date	Hour	Summary of Events and Information	Remarks and references to Appendices
St Elm H2	20.5.17		Night Targets D3d 93.05. D3d 28.55. D9c 78.48. D9c 85.65. B/190 92/Hrs. 4 guns A/190 from H35c 65.90 & H35c 40.30.	
	21.5.17		Wire cutting proceeding on extreme left of Divisional front by C/190 dich. Enemy shelling very quiet during the day. A few 7.7 shrapnel were fired over the new Overland route crossing the Diekebusch road N.E. of that village. At 9.55 P.M. heavy shelling on our front on both flanks. We retaliated twice at the request of Infantry — all quiet at 10.45 P.M. Bombardment on our left started again on our left at 3.45 A.M. died down again. Our front Normal during the night. Night targets on Trench junctions strong points 504 & Bt. 2 Hours.	
	22.5.17		Wet day very quiet during the morning, weather improved during the afternoon MTM's with enemy fire ensued to cut wire at 4 P.M. to 4.20 P.M. C/190 cut wire from RUINED FARM to the left but had to stop owing to Hostile Aeroplanes patrolling the line. 10 P.M. heavy barrage on our front line supports — group artillery stood to but were not called upon to fire except retaliation by D/190	

T2134. Wt. W708-776. 500000. 4/15. Sir J. C. & S.

Army Form C. 2118.

WAR DIARY
INTELLIGENCE SUMMARY.
(Erase heading not required.)

190th Bde R.F.A.

Instructions regarding War Diaries and Intelligence Summaries are contained in F. S. Regs., Part II. and the Staff Manual respectively. Title pages will be prepared in manuscript.

Place	Date	Hour	Summary of Events and Information	Remarks and references to Appendices
St Eloi H.2	22.5.17		Night firing by B/190 on new trenches & strong point. Enemy shelling very quiet. M.T.M's cut wire as usual with covering fire. C/190 cut wire N. of RUINED FARM.	
	23.5.17		Night firing by A/190 on points bombarded during the day by the 1st Corps H.A.	
	24.5.17		VOORMEZEELE front line shelled throughout the day. C/190 cut wire as usual N.E. of Ruined Farm. Night firing by B/190. Major G. Neame RFA listed to command B/190. Hostile artillery very active from 8am to 11am N. of Canal. C/190 heavily shelled with S.G's. 1 gun knocked out & 1 temporarily out of action. 4 O.R's wounded. B/190 at N4d85.70 shelled between 7 & 9am with 42 guns, no damage to men or material except 1 O.R wounded.	
	25.5.17		Enemy fire again provoked by B/190 for M.T.M's cutting wire. Night firing by 504th Bty. 466th Bty took up position at H35c65.90.	
	26.5.17		Enemy shelling very active all day. Café Belge, Ridgewood & Tunnel	

T2134. Wt. W708—776. 500000. 4/16. Sir J. C. & S.

Army Form C. 2118.

WAR DIARY
INTELLIGENCE SUMMARY.
(Erase heading not required.)

190th - Bde RFA.

Place	Date	Hour	Summary of Events and Information	Remarks and references to Appendices
Eccles H.2	26.5.17		Back areas. M.T.M's cut wire with exemy fire from B/190.	
			D/190 fired 100 rds in destroying new work O8b5½5	
			Night firing - A/190.	
			504th Bty moved to B1. H35c 50.65.	
			D/190 7 Section do A2. H35c 55.05.	
			40th Bty do E5. H36c 10.85.	
			A/187 do C3	
			1 gun C/72 do F1	
			1 gun B/72 do F2	
	27.5.17		Enemy started shelling Braeme (H29c) with 5.9c + 8 inch APiercing	
		5.30 am to 9 am	again a few rounds at noon.	
			New Batteries registered their 3 wires during the day	
		4 PM	D/190 fired 200 rds on trenches O8d 5½ 3	
		9.30 PM	heavy shelling on our right - also on our front - increased	
			in intensity about 10.30 PM. Ceased altogether at 11.45 PM. enemy	
			had been heavily shelling Ridge Wood, Muighbury Ride trenches	

Army Form C. 2118.

WAR DIARY
~~INTELLIGENCE SUMMARY~~   190th Bde RFA

(Erase heading not required.)

Instructions regarding War Diaries and Intelligence Summaries are contained in F. S. Regs., Part II. and the Staff Manual respectively. Title pages will be prepared in manuscript.

Place	Date	Hour	Summary of Events and Information	Remarks and references to Appendices
Seli #2	27.5.17		6/190 move to H346 15. while digging new position A4 N5 & 76.30.	
			465th Bty moved into position at B3.	
			D/190 1 Section do do A2.	
			40th " do do E5.	
			B/187 do do C2.	
			D/72 do do B5.	
			A/52 do do D1.	
			2 am all roads, Batteries, tracks etc in area heavily shelled with gas & tear shell. Traffic disorganised on roads. Many men slightly gassed & treated at these H.Q. by the M.O. This continued till 5 am, when enemy kept up a slow rate of fire of S.9. 4.2's 9 4.2 guns in Batteries around. 30 RS gassed. 1 wounded. 2/Lt C.H. Loughnan from Reinforcements posted to D/190.	
	28.5.17		# Col G Symonds 187 Bde RFA takes over command of Northern Group.	
			~~#~~ T/Col G.A Curtis DSO 190th Bde RFA do do Southern Group.	
			41st Divl Arty the dividing line being O2c 77.92.	
			Batteries continue to register the new zone	

WAR DIARY
or
INTELLIGENCE SUMMARY.
(Erase heading not required.)

Army Form C. 2118.

190th Bde R.F.A.

Place	Date	Hour	Summary of Events and Information	Remarks and references to Appendices
Southern group S.E.01	29.5.17		B/190 cut wire on left of Dinainel & one with forward gun. At noon this group. handed covering fire for M.T.M.'s cutting wire on left of Crater. Large programme of day & night firing for all Batteries ordered in connection with coming offensive, impossible to give all details of targets and ammunition.	
	30.5.17	11.30 am	a Practice Barrage for A. B. & C. Groups 41st D.A. in conjunction with IX th Corps on our right, this was judged most effective. A raid took place at 3.10 am 30/31st – no identification obtained. Usual day & night firing.	
	31.5.17		Concentrated shoot by M.T.M.'s on Crater area with covering fire from the group at 5 PM to 5.30 PM. Lt K.N. Findlay B/190 posted to B Echelon 41st DAC & Lt D. Vyle posted to B/190 in exchange. Usual day & night bombardments, enemy shelled back areas with gas shell.	Effective fire

T2134. Wt. W708—776. 500000. 4/15. Sir J. C. & S.

WAR DIARY

INTELLIGENCE SUMMARY

41st D.A.
190th Bde R.F.A.

Army Form C. 2118.

Place	Date	Hour	Summary of Events and Information	Remarks and references to Appendices
A.6 y a.f. H21 41st D.A. H28 d 7.8.	1.6.17		Heavy Bombardments, Practice Barrages, day & night firing, continue; enemy retaliation slight – usually consisting of shelling our back areas & communication by night with gas shells & Howitzers with instantaneous fuzes, he succeeded in blowing up several dumps of ammunition already in place for the coming Offensive on the front. Some guns damaged also but few casualties to this Brigade. Systematic Bombardment for "V" day taken place today.	
	2.6.17		"W" day Bombardment continues. Lt. & J.S.C. Peile C/190 killed during the night by direct hit on his dug out. Lt. F.M.V. Earle C/190 slightly gassed at the same time. Successful raid by 122nd Inf. Bde at 10 PM. 6 prisoners – 1 M. Gun + a telephone taken. Artillery supplied by this Group reported excellent. Heavy programme of Bombardments night firing etc. take place for the coming Offensive.	

Army Form C. 2118.

WAR DIARY
or
INTELLIGENCE SUMMARY.
(Erase heading not required.)

190th Bde RFA.

Instructions regarding War Diaries and Intelligence Summaries are contained in F.S. Regs., Part II. and the Staff Manual respectively. Title pages will be prepared in manuscript.

Place	Date	Hour	Summary of Events and Information	Remarks and references to Appendices
Agny H.2	3.6.17		Preparation & bombardments continue.	
	4.6.17		do	
	5.6.17		do	
	6.6.17		do	
	7.6.17		Zero hour for Attack at 3.10am. Before this time enemy shelled back areas with gas shell. Punctually to time the barrage started. As far as the army front were touched off the Barrage. Objective was taken at the Divison was concerned enemy reported time there was little at all - Batteries kept well to their programme continuous fire was maintained for over 6 hours. A/190 advanced to new position at 10.40am B/190 do 12.15 P.M. Both got up without any incident. During the Operation Major G.S. Sweetapple DSO. RFA D/190 was acting as Stan Liaison Officer with the 124th Inf Bde. Lt E.H.R. Farrell RFA D/190 was with the 11th Battn Queens Regt. Both reached	

Army Form C. 2118.

WAR DIARY
or
INTELLIGENCE SUMMARY.
(Erase heading not required.)

190th - Bde RFA

Place	Date	Hour	Summary of Events and Information	Remarks and references to Appendices
			valuable help rendered by sending messages back to the Group HQ which were transmitted to D.A. HQ	
			2/Lt. G.D. Doyle RFA A/190 with Signaller went forward with the order to register the Batteries as they advanced to the new positions. Owing to bad communication he was unable to accomplish anything until the evening but he sent back valuable information collected German before it. He with No.73568 Bdr. T.D. Nagle, alone captured 16 prisoners, a machine gun (the number included 1 Officer & 1 Sergeant) They were recommended for immediate award.	as F.O.O.
			Bde H.Q. moved in the afternoon to MOATED GRANGE D.1.a.6.4. just behind the Batteries	
8.6.17			C/190 moved up early this morning 2D/190 during night 8/9 June. Net result of Offensive - the whole of Wytschaete - Messines Ridge was taken with over 20 guns more than 8000 prisoners	
9.6.17			Consolidation - Registration of new country - selection of O.P's & settling into new positions	
10.6.17				

WAR DIARY

190 Bde RFA

Army Form C. 2118.

Place	Date	Hour	Summary of Events and Information	Remarks and references to Appendices
D.1.a.6.4.	11.6.17		Further Registration by all Batteries. – a certain amount of night firing & harassing fire was carried out.	
	12/6		Enemy shelled VOORMEZEELE roads towards new tracks each night, & appeared to be getting new Batteries into position opposite our front to replace those captured & destroyed by us in 2nd attack on June 7.	
	13/6			
	14/6			
	15/6			
	16/6		On 14th inst. this Brigade assisted to cover 122nd Inf. Bde. in taking the remainder of Opts 7 trench – there was authority & in consequence we were able to get a better view of the ground into foreground of HOLLEBEKE Village which was impossible before owing to the formation of the ground.	
	17/6			
	18/6			
T.31.C.45.30	19		Headquarters changed place with 65th AFA Bde. moved to VOORMEZEELE	
	20		Nothing to report	
	21 22		A/277 & B/277 were withdrawn to their wagon lines & #1 Section D/277 moved & took up position vacated by 277th Bde. A/190 2nd Section D/190	
	23			
	24		B/277 was withdrawn. D/190 moved their remaining guns.	
	2.45am		Creeping Barrage by the whole Group, lasting 12 minutes, over the ground East & West of HOLLEBEKE Village to catch ration parties & machine

Army Form C. 2118.

WAR DIARY
or
INTELLIGENCE SUMMARY.
(Erase heading not required.)

190th Bde RFA.

Place	Date	Hour	Summary of Events and Information	Remarks and references to Appendices
I31c45.30	24		Guns sited in Shell-holes. No retaliation, 1OR killed 1 wounded at H.2.	
	25		C/277 moved to Wagon Lines. Position left empty.	
			H.2. moved to hostile Barrage early in the morning to avoid the counter attack shelling which was received by VOORMEZEELE daily.	
			Enemy began shelling tracks about 4.30 P.M. most vigorously with all sorts of Howitzers, including 8 inch with instantaneous fuse many of which fell on & near MOATED GRANGE, so H.2 moved again that night to vicinity of ELZENWALLE about H36c3.1.	
H36c3.1.	26		Enemy shelled all tracks and back areas by day & sprinkled them with Shrapnel at night. Hostile aeroplanes very active each day.	
	27		Counter quite low & enemy ow Observation balloons frequently.	
	28		Our fire during this period limited almost entirely to Retaliation on	
	29		soft points in enemy lines	
	30			

APMurth
Lt Col RFA
Comdg 190th Bde RFA

WAR DIARY or INTELLIGENCE SUMMARY

Army Form C. 2118.

190th Bde RFA

Vol/5

Place	Date	Hour	Summary of Events and Information	Remarks and references to Appendices
T31 c 45 30	1.7.17		41st D.A. handed over to 47th D.A. today at 9 a.m. This Brigade will go out of the line to rest with the 41st Division in a few days time. Has position at T32d 80.42 started this morning - 5 men Batteries being supplied for this purpose. Strayshell killed 2 & wounded 1 O.R.s while they were starting to dig, both all of A/190.	
	2.7.17		Cold Trust - no firing beyond registration by A & D/190 of the country North of Canal	
	3.7.17			
	4.7.17		This brigade at 9 a.m. form the Oosthock group. Thirteen the Divisional front which runs from the KLEIN ZILLEBEKE road to O.11 a 2.2. Liaison duties are now found by the two other Groups, B E 101 & the Battle Wood group - in future we only find when relieved by 47th D.A. to reinforce some part of the line. Nothing to report.	
	5.7.17			
	6.7.17		Brigade relieved by 26th Army Bde RFA	
	7.7.17		marched from Wagon lines to rest area near FLETRE.	
	8.7.17 to 20.7.17		Brigade at rest. Nothing to report. 2/Lt E.O. Doyle A/190 granted the MILITARY CROSS for conspicuous gallantry in the attack on June 7th when he acted as Brigade F.O.O.	

Army Form C. 2118.

WAR DIARY
or
INTELLIGENCE SUMMARY.
(Erase heading not required.)

190th Bde R.F.A.

Instructions regarding War Diaries and Intelligence Summaries are contained in F. S. Regs., Part II. and the Staff Manual respectively. Title pages will be prepared in manuscript.

Place	Date	Hour	Summary of Events and Information	Remarks and references to Appendices
O.1.b.6.95.	21.7.17		Brigade marched back into action taking back their old guns from 26th Bde - Headquarters moved into dugouts at O.1.b.60.95. Two Australian Batteries 41st & 111th came into the Group which was called Oostitoek Group. Preparations continued for the coming attack.	
	22.7.17		B/190 & 41st Batteries were made Silent Batteries. the remaining 4 Batteries took it in turns to carry out Day & Night firing. The consisted of about 100 rds 18 Pr, & from 50-200 rds How. Harassing fire at night & about 50 rds 18 Pr, & 50 rds How searching shell-holes in front of our own line by day.	
	23/7		}	
	24/7		} Dumps were maintained of 1300 rds per 18 Pr & 1100 rds per 4.5 How.	
	25/7		} Nothing of importance took part. Hostile shelling varied during	
	26/7		} this time - a large amount of gas shell was used at night by	
	27/7		} the enemy also by us.	
	28.7.17		Captain C.F. Farrell R.F.A. O/190 left to be second in command of "T" Battery 14th Army Bde R.H.A. 2Lt A.K. Andrews A/190 wounded.	

A6945 Wt. W1427/M160 35,000 12/16 D. D. & L. Forms/C./2118/14.

Army Form C. 2118.

WAR DIARY
or
INTELLIGENCE SUMMARY.
(Erase heading not required.)

190th Bde RFA

Place	Date	Hour	Summary of Events and Information	Remarks and references to Appendices
O,26.095	29.7.17		2/Lt E.D Doyle RFA A/190 was killed this morning by a chance shell on his dug out. M.C.	
	30.7.17		Heavy enemy shelling of back areas with unusually heavy Howitzers. Zero day fixed for the 31st	
	31.7.17		Zero hour 3.50 am - visibility very poor owing to low clouds. Attack started in the dark - several points machine guns held up the Infantry on more than one occasion there were dealt with by the 4.5 hows of this Brigade notably on the Canal bank east & North east of HOLLEBEKE village. 9~ front of the Group attack goes well, further north it is hung up by machine guns in several areas heavy counter attacks driven off several times during the day following night. Relieving Capt G.K. Jenkins RFA posted to command D/190 Term. The acting Bridge of Major vice Major G.S. Lunthorpe D.S.O. RFA posted to 2nd Army Art. School TILQUES. (2.7.17.)	
	23.7.17		Capt Twine RFA from H.Q. D.A.H.Q. to be 2nd in command of	

WAR DIARY
or
INTELLIGENCE SUMMARY.

Army Form C. 2118.

190th Bde RFA

Place	Date	Hour	Summary of Events and Information	Remarks and references to Appendices
Postings contd.		D/190	vice Capt. G. H. Oakes posted to Base Reinforcements Havre.	

W Morris Lt Col. RFA
190 Bde RFA
Commanding 190 Bde RFA

To Headquarters,

    41st Divisional Artillery.

Herewith War Diary for the month of August 1917.

2-9-1917.

                                           Lieutenant Colonel. R.F.A.
                                    Commanding 190th Brigade., R.F.A.

WAR DIARY
INTELLIGENCE SUMMARY

Army Form C. 2118.

190th Bde RFA

Oct 16

Place	Date	Hour	Summary of Events and Information	Remarks
O.16.b.95	1.8.17		Weather breaks up, stops all active operations — continual rain & low visibility, light then from taken — continual shelling of Brigade Battery positions, platforms become very wet & there is much discomfort in all positions.	
	2.8.17			
	3.8.17			
	4.8.17		Weather improves slightly, but more rain falls in afternoon.	
	5.8.17		Rain stops but visibility however keeps the enemy who come over under its protection managing to get a footing in our line east of Hollebeke village & Forret Farm. He is at once driven out. TMB Barrage stops him bringing up reinforcements. Enemy repeats his morning efforts at 9.35 p.m. but were again met by Barrage come right down & hove him down — our heavy guns also fire in his back areas. Large amount of ammunition fired in organised Night firing by all Batteries — searching positions in bursts.	

A6045 Wt. W11422/M1160 35.000 12/16. D. D. & L. Forms/C./2118/14.

WAR DIARY
or
INTELLIGENCE SUMMARY.
(Erase heading not required.)

Army Form C. 2118.

190th Bde RFA

Place	Date	Hour	Summary of Events and Information	Remarks and references to Appendices
01.66.09.5	5.8.17		In front of our front line.	
			4th Lt J.H. Austin, Battn. have we section ordr to the Wagon Lines	
	6.8.17	(4.8.17) 2nd Lt Keates & 2nd Lt J.S. Ferguson D/190 wounded in action. Nothing to report	
	7.8.17	2nd Lt J.V. Symons joined from 19th D.A.C. posted to A/190 2nd Lt J. Harland joined, posted to D/190. 2nd Lt C.W. Anderson transferred from 41st D.A.C. posted to C/190 2nd Lt Helm do A/190 Night firing took the form of the 4.5 How bombarding the Canal & Railway embankment while the 18Pr put up a Barrage 50yds S.W. of the. This shoot took place at 2.40am lasting till 3.10am	
	8.8.17	was repeated at 4.8 am 2nd Lt Anderson & 2nd Lt Helm reported to 41st D.A.C. 2nd Lt B. Middleton joined from 14th Division - posted to A/190. 2nd Lt T.E. Wheate do B/190.	

Army Form C. 2118.

WAR DIARY
or
INTELLIGENCE SUMMARY.

(Erase heading not required.)

190 Bde R.F.A.

Place	Date	Hour	Summary of Events and Information	Remarks and references to Appendices
01.b.60.95	8.8.17		2Lt. H.S. French posted from 41st D.A.C. to C/190.	
			2Lt. E. De Pierres " " " 14th Division to D/190.	
	9.8.17	at 4.35	A+B/190 fired barrage on S.O.S. lines until 6 lifts of 100yds each for 1 hour	
			D/190 engaged M.G's at 06d 7.8 for 5 minutes, the bombardment POTSDAM FARM for 55 minutes.	
			The above operation took place to support the IInd Corps in an Left in their attack.	
	10/8			
	11/8		360 rds 18 Pr. fired in unrestricted shoots on selected points each	
	12/8		day & 300 rds fired each night in bursts on tracks & communications behind the enemy's lines.	
	13/8		On the night 12/13th D/190 fired 324 rds lethal & 66 H.E. on P.7.a 05.30 D/190 moved 1 Section of Hows to new position at O.3.d 0.5 on night 11/12 & 1 Section Q/B. actual A/190 to be acting Major on whilst in command of a 6.g 4m Captain Q/B. actual A/190 to be acting Major on whilst in command of a 6.g 4m	
	14/8		Battery A/190 vir major Arnold M.C. evacuated dated 24.7.17.	

Army Form C. 2118.

WAR DIARY
INTELLIGENCE SUMMARY.
(Erase heading not required.)

190th Bde RFA

Place	Date	Hour	Summary of Events and Information	Remarks and references to Appendices
O.B. 6095	14/8		Lt. V.A. MACKENZIE promoted to rank of Captain without pay or allowances whilst performing the duties of Adjutant with effect from 12.8.17	
	15/8		2/Lt. V.T. Verfeld joined from Reinforcements posted to B/190.	
			2/Lt. F. Sheridan do do C/190.	
	16/8		Nothing of importance beyond usual day and night firing.	
	17/8			
	18/8		36623 A/Bdr. D. Smith D/190 awarded MILITARY MEDAL	
			36742 Gnr. F. Hutton do do	
	19/8		Lt. M. Thompson B/190 transferred to A/190 & promoted A/Capt whilst 2nd in Command of that Battery.	
			2/Lt. De Pierres transferred from D/190 to C/190.	
	20/8		Sergt. W.G. Sellar (1217) C/190 awarded the MILITARY MEDAL	
			Lt. R. Young from 14th A. Bde. RHA attached to B/190.	
			Lt. A.S. Borthwick returned from 2nd Army Signal Course attached to D/190.	
	21/8		D/190 has been into the Tactical command of Canal Group	
	21/8		At 7am all Batteries cooperated with an attack by IInd Corps	

Army Form C. 2118.

WAR DIARY
INTELLIGENCE SUMMARY.

190 Bde RFA

(Erase heading not required.)

Place	Date	Hour	Summary of Events and Information	Remarks and references to Appendices
O.18.b.0.9.5	22/8		Dy firing a barrage on S.O.S. lines advancing in 6 lifts of 100 yds each lift for 3 minutes rates of fire - Zero to 3 plus 2, 4 rds per gun per minute. 3 to plus 2 to Zero plus 20, 2 rds per gun per minute. 1 Section per Battery withdrew when barrage lines A/190 being relieved by	
	23/8		A/119 - the remainder leaving their positions vacant	
	24/8		H.Q. remainder of Bde (A B C) withdrew to Bergen lines	
	25/8		H.Q. A Bde C/190 marched to Boche area en route for 41st Divn moved next area	
	26/8		March continued to villages of Val d'Acquin & Westbecourt - West of S. Omer.	
			2 Lts Howland & Kirkham proceeded to 2nd Army Arty. School for a Course.	
	27/8		Lt Young B/190 transferred to A/190	
			Lt Russell A/190 do B/190.	
	28/		Very wet stormy - no drill.	
	29/		Colonel Carden leave to Boulogne 27 - 30.	
	30/		Capt Welch C/190 proceeded Bergues to 1st Hirt 47 & DAC on 29th	
	31/			

HJ Jackson
Commanding 190 Bde RFA

To Headquarters
41st Division ~~Artillery~~

Herewith War Diary
for November 1917

3/12/17   A. Murdoch Lt Colonel R.H.A.
             Commanding 190 Bde R.H.A.

Army Form C. 2118

WAR DIARY
or
INTELLIGENCE SUMMARY

(Erase heading not required.)

190 Bde RFA

Vol 17

Instructions regarding War Diaries and Intelligence Summaries are contained in F. S. Regs., Part II. and the Staff Manual respectively. Title Pages will be prepared in manuscript.

Place	Date	Hour	Summary of Events and Information	Remarks and references to Appendices
Westrecout	1/9			
	2/9		Nothing to report. 2/Lt W. Hanragen C/190 appointed Second in command of C/190 2.9.17 with acting rank of Captain.	
	3/9		do	
	4/9		do	
	5/9		Brigade handed to GODEWAERSVELDE on thirteenth to the line.	
	6/9		do Dickebusch area to wagon lines.	
	7/9		Nothing to report, beyond Batteries sent of working parties to dig positions near HILL 60.	
	8/9		1 section each of A + B/190 relieved 1 section of 13th + 14th Australian Batteries respectively, came under 23rd D.A. for defence of the line. Remainder of relief above was completed. 2/Lt L.H. Peadeth C/190 attached to B/190.	
	9/9		Nothing to report	
	10/9		1 Section each of C/190 & D/190 occupied their new positions	
	11/9			
	12/9		Remainder of C/190 & D/190 went into action.	
	13/9			

Army Form C. 2118

190th — Bde RFA

WAR DIARY
or
INTELLIGENCE SUMMARY
(Erase heading not required.)

Instructions regarding War Diaries and Intelligence Summaries are contained in F. S. Regs., Part II. and the Staff Manual respectively. Title Pages will be prepared in manuscript.

Place	Date	Hour	Summary of Events and Information	Remarks and references to Appendices
H33d8.3.	13/9		Headquarters moved up to LARCH WOOD TUNNELS South (I29c6.4.) defence of the line still with 23rd D.A. — we receive orders for coming Offensive	
I29c.6.4	14/9		All Batteries to be in their Battle positions by this date — A B O C/94 Batteries come under the front for Offensive action — the front is called Southern front 41 D.A. consists of 7 Batteries — 6, 8 P.O. 91, 45 Hows Two O.P.s arranged for the front (a) Concrete dugout at J25b 30.78. 9(b) Steel Camouflage tree near Lone Stw Post J25b 10.10. South front Zone from J19d 48.05 — J27a 45.26.8 J25b 26.00 — J26d 68.91. Harassing fire takes place as follows over the Zone each night by 18P.O. on certain hundred targets at the rate of 25 rds per task per hour	
	19/9		4.5 Hows with Gas on 14th, 16th, & 18th without gas on 15th, 17th, 19th on specified targets.	

Army Form C. 2118.

WAR DIARY
or
INTELLIGENCE SUMMARY.
(Erase heading not required.)

190 Bde RFA

Place	Date	Hour	Summary of Events and Information	Remarks and references to Appendices
Izel le H.	14/9 to 19/9 cont.		Preparation Barrages were fired as under one fired in each time by a Battery Commander:—	
	September	15th 8 am	Cnfs Barrage No 4	
		4 P.M.	do No. 3	
		16th 10 am	Army Barrage No 1	
		6 P.M.	Cnfs Barrage No 2	
		17th 6 am	do do repeated	
		3 P.M.	do No. 1	
		18th 6 am	Army Barrage No. 2	
		8.30 am	do No. 3	
		19th 3 P.M.	Cnfs Barrage as for attack dw.	
			Liaison Officers were detailed as follows for attack dw.	
			Captain W. Harrison C/190 with 124th Inf Bde.	
			2nd L. R. Hilden A/94 do Rt. Battalion in the attack	
			Lt. C. H. Ingham D/190 do left do do	
			Lt R.A.H.S. Geddes B/94 & Lt. G.D. Gole D/190 were heart as front F.O.O.'s on	

WAR DIARY
or
INTELLIGENCE SUMMARY.
(Erase heading not required.)

Army Form C. 2118.

190 Bde RFA.

Place	Date	Hour	Summary of Events and Information	Remarks and references to Appendices
T29c6	20/9		Attack took place at 5.40am with good weather conditions after some rain during the night. Objectives were all taken by L/F Bde of this Division, but the 124 Bde had trouble with machine gun fire from enemy dugouts directly in front which caused casualties. Held up the advance. By 2.30 PM "Blue line" had been consolidated — our rates of fire considerable reduced. At 6.30 PM enemy launched a heavy counter attack against our front but prompt assistance by all Batteries in the group broke up their formation.	
	21/9		At 4.30am a preparatory Barrage lasting for 45 minutes. Batteries fired down on the group zone — no certain known enemy tracks TOFs at night on SOS line. Barrages took place at 5am & 7PM as before — Day & night firing as for 21st	
	22/9			
	23/9		Barrages were fired at 7.30 PM. Day firing on tracks — night firing but enemy shelling during these days was heavy over the Battery area	

Army Form C. 2118.

WAR DIARY
or
INTELLIGENCE SUMMARY.
(Erase heading not required.)

190 Bde RFA

Place	Date	Hour	Summary of Events and Information	Remarks and references to Appendices
Trgc 6.4 H33 d 8.3.	24/9	8 am	Barrage fired at 8 am.	
	25/9		Group H.Q. relieved by 94th Bde during the day. — 2nd Lt Boyd D.S.O. taken over command at 6 P.M. — 190 Bde H.Q. withdrew to wagon lines. Battery fired Barrages at 6 am & at 2.15 P.M.	
	26/9		Batteries took part in attack on the day, no details to hand.	
	27/9		2 Sections per Battery came out of action in the evening	
	28/9		do do in the morning	
			Battery Cmdrs reconnoitred positions South of MENIN RD & J.13 c 9 d for an attack East of POLYGON WOOD. Have been shelling in the neighbourhood.	
	29/9		Working parties from Batteries started work on new positions. Ammunition sent up by Batteries & D.A.C. in pubs.	
	30/9		Supply of Ammunition & Batteries positions continued. Casualties. 1st G.D. Gale D/190. wounded 20.9.17. Major E. Brandish A/190 wounded 27.9.17 (remained at duty) 2nd Lt. E. De Pierres C/190 died of wounds 17.9.17 2nd Lt. M.V. Rowe B/190 gassed 19.9.17.	

Army Form C. 2118.

WAR DIARY
or
INTELLIGENCE SUMMARY
(Erase heading not required.)

190ᵗʰ Bde RFA

Place	Date	Hour	Summary of Events and Information	Remarks and references to Appendices
			<u>Casualties for the month of September 17 continued</u>	
			O.R's. killed 18, wounded 39.	
			2/Lt. G. Booth with from D/190 to be attached to B/190. 16/9/17.	
			2/Lt. J.V. Symonds from A/190 do C/190 16/9/17	

W Garden
Lt Col RFA
Commanding 190ᵗʰ Bde RFA

Army Form C. 2118.

190th Bde R.F.A.

9/07/18

WAR DIARY
INTELLIGENCE SUMMARY.
(Erase heading not required.)

Place	Date	Hour	Summary of Events and Information	Remarks and references to Appendices
H33 d 8.3. I23 a 60.65	1/10/17		Bde Headquarters moved to DORMY HOUSE (Map ref as per margin) took command of left group 21st D.A. consisting of 190 Bde & B & 9/95th Bde R.F.A. Group continued preparation for attack (see 21 D.A. O.O. No. 87). By this night all batteries were in action but were not responsible for holding the line.	
			Captain M. Thompson A/190 severely wounded in taking up ammunition 2 Lt P.S. Preston H.2. 190 do	
	2/10/17		Battery positions heavily shelled at 7 P.M., all lines out, no casualties to personnel	
			Took over defence of the line at 8 P.M. (in the middle of a call for S.O.S) S.O.S. at 5.30 am	
	3/10/17		Practice Barrage at 6 am — followed by very heavy shelling of Battery positions lasting till about noon — every line being again cut to bits Practice Barrage at 3 P.M.	
			2 Lt J. Q. Sexton joined from Reinforcements posted to B/190. 1/10/17	
	4/10/17		We attacked at 6 am. Though held up in the centre for a time, took all	

Army Form C. 2118.

WAR DIARY
or
INTELLIGENCE SUMMARY.
(Erase heading not required.)

190 Bde RFA

Place	Date	Hour	Summary of Events and Information	Remarks and references to Appendices
Essaboeufs	4/10		Our objectives. Enemy shelling was quite wild during the first hours of the attack, but later was very heavy on the Battery positions.	
	5/10		C/190 handed 1 gun to B/149. Rest of Brigade (A/B) were relieved by Batteries of 21st Division & HQ 95 Bde RFA withdrew from the area.	
	6/10		Prepared to march from the area.	
	7/10		Marched to ZERMEZEELE en route for 4th Army area.	
	8/10		Marched to St Pol (near DUNKIRK) remained in 4th Army area without orders to report.	
	9/10			
	10/10			
	11/10		10 Officers & 2 men per HQ & Batteries proceeded by lorry to learn the front occupied by 41st & 34th Divisions & to take over Battery positions from 210th Bde XVth Corps.	
	12/10		} Nothing to report.	
	13/10			
	14/10			

Army Form C. 2118.

WAR DIARY
or
INTELLIGENCE SUMMARY.
(Erase heading not required.)

190th Bde RFA

Instructions regarding War Diaries and Intelligence Summaries are contained in F. S. Regs., Part II. and the Staff Manual respectively. Title pages will be prepared in manuscript.

Place	Date	Hour	Summary of Events and Information	Remarks and references to Appendices
Coxyde Bains	15/10		Brigade marched to wagon lines about COXYDE BAINS.	
	16/10		1 Section and Battery relieved Battens. 158 Q. Bde RFA & D/210th Bde.	
	17/10		Remainder of relief complete at night.	
			2Lt. BINNIE joined from Reinforcements attached to D/190.	
			2Lt. WARD do A/190	
(Sheet 11 S.E.)				
R29c7.4.	18/10		Headquarters took over from 158th Bde returned command of A Group	
			Lt. DA.	
			Lt. Col. G.A. CARDEW DSO. RFA. proceeded on one month leave to England.	
			MAJOR J.C. O'CALLAGHAN MC RFA. C/190 assumed command of Brigade.	
			BSM. GIBBS W.J. A/190 awarded "MILITARY CROSS" for GALLANTRY in the FIELD. 10.10.17.	
	19/10		Major G. NEAME B/190 awarded MILITARY CROSS do	
			Major R. BRANDISH A/190 do do	
		No. 14290	BSM. WHARTON A.E. C/190 do D.C.M.	
			Enemy shells heap square M19d which includes A.B.& D Battery positions	
	20/10-26/10		Nothing to report beyond usual enemy shelling of our positions, & AEOLIAN ROAD.	

Army Form C. 2118.

WAR DIARY
INTELLIGENCE SUMMARY.
(Erase heading not required.)

190th Bde RFA

Place	Date	Hour	Summary of Events and Information	Remarks and references to Appendices
R.29 & 74	28/10	9 am	Received orders to hand over to 51st Bde 9th Div. that night & following night & withdraw to Ghyvelde area.	
	29/10		Handed over command of Group to 51st Bde. Batteries were also relieved & withdrew to Ghyvelde at night.	
	30/10		Brigade taken steps to reequip completely, up to Mobilisation table, in order to proceed by train to ITALY under XIVth Corps in a few days time.	
	31/10		Driving drill, Gun drill & signalling taken place daily. Forwarding of heavier equipment. All ranks warned for to return from leave on the 29th. Lt. Col. G.A. CARDEN D.S.O. reassumes command on the 31st on his return from leave.	

B.Y. Jackson Major RFA
Cmdg 190 Bde RFA

To Headquarters,

    41st Divisional Artillery.

    Herewith War Diary of this Brigade for the month of October.

31-10-17.   Lieutenant Colonel. R.F.A.
                                                     Commanding 190th Brigade., R.F.A.

WO 95/2625/6
41 DIV
190 BDE RFA
MARCH 1918 - OCT 1919

41st Div.

Bde. returned with
Div. from Italy
8/12.3.18.

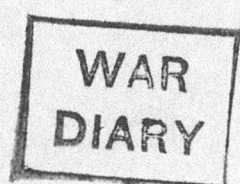

Headquarters,

190th BRIGADE, R.F.A.

M A R C H

1 9 1 8

Place	Date	Hour	Summary of Events and Information	Remarks and references to Appendices
SOVILLA	1/3		2/Lt G.T. HODGSON transferred from C/190 to B/190. D/190 came out of action this night on the left of MONTELLO & went into action in their new position near Road 2.	
	2/3		Lt H. DOBINSON M.C. A/190 transferred to the 23rd D.A.	
	3/3		Nothing to report.	
	4/3		Notified that 5th Divisional Operations were strandured owing to bad weather. D/190 withdrew to wagon line at night.	
	5/3		Headquarters & Batteries marched to PAESE area, parties from CAZZELLE also marched & joined up at ST PAESE. Lt Col G.A. CARDEW returned from England. Prepared to entrain for return to France.	
	6/3 7/3 8/3 9/3 10/3		Brigade entrained at TREVISO Centrale. In the train.	
	11/3 12/3		Brigade detrained at DOULLENS & went into Billets as follows.	

Place	Date	Hour	Summary of Events and Information	Remarks and references to Appendices
GÉZAINCOURT			H.Q. Bde/igo at GÉZAINCOURT. A 2C/igo at GOUCHEZ.	
	13/3		Nothing to report.	
	14/3		Lt.Col Carter C.M.G. D.S.O. went with the C.R.A. to visit the IV th Corps area	
	15/3		Nothing to report. Capt. W.A. Mackenzie took over duties of Staff Captain R.A. on Captain Bischoff proceeding on leave to U.K. Lt. R Penney took over duties of Adjutant for same reason.	
	16/3		Nothing to report beyond overhauling of equipment guns etc.	
	20/3		Bugde marched to CONTAY area — heavy bombardment and attack by enemy on IV th Corps Front.	
CONTAY	21/3		Order received to march to BUIRE area. Subsequently cancelled & marched to ABLAINZEVILLE — arriving in afternoon in camp, marched off to action in evening owing to IV th Corps being heavily engaged by	
ABLAINZEVILLE	22/3		enemy attack — taking up position north of FAVREUIL village covering the green line & 3rd line of defence. 4.1st Divisional Artillery moved with drawal of 6th Division who fell back conforming with the	

Place	Date	Hour	Summary of Events and Information
FAVREUIL	24/3	*	Batteries retired from positions SOUTH of SAPIGNIES & North of BIHUCOURT
	22/3		troops on either flank. Captain W.A. Mackay - reported to Bde as adjutant, on afternoon of 23rd. Lt.Col Carter acting in closest liaison with G.O.C. 124th Inf Bde decided to withdraw by alternate Brigades to positions SOUTH of SAPIGNIES 93rd Bde moved first then 190th Bde then 110th Bde. Bde H.Q. moved to huts S.W. of BIHUCOURT from dugouts in FAVREUIL Wood
	25/3	†	Enemy still attacking in force, orders were received to withdraw again to conform with troops on Right who had now retired from BAPAUME. Alternate Batteries of Bde retired to positions West of ACHIET-LE-GRAND Railway. Bde H.Q. moved to huts on Rd. West of ACHIET-LE-PETIT At night (11 PM) Battalion came into action near CRUCIFIX North of BUCQUOY - 124th Bde being relieved by 185th Bde (62nd Div) Liaison was established with G.O.C. of that Bde
	26/3		At 4 am Bde moved back to positions West of ESSARTS, Bde H.Q. being in ESSARTS village - infantry holding line 1000 yds East of BUCQUOY finally falling back to outskirts of that village.

Place	Date	Hour	Summary of Events and Information	Remarks and references to Appces
ESSARTS	26/3		110th Bde. left than Group, the 312th Bde being allotted in place. 93rd Bde left than Group. An exact account of foregoing incidents is impossible to record owing to the constant movement. Brigade behaved splendidly throughout these Operations - all movements being carried out with great care & precision. Some incidents should be mentioned hereunder eg (a), 1 Section D/190 remaining behind on the BAPAUME - ARRAS Road till the Infantry retired on them, digging trenches beside the guns which only retired when their ammunition was exhausted. (b) Lt. I.E. HUMPHREYS A/190 acting as Battn. Liason Officer did not excellent work with the 124th Ind. Bde & the 185th Inf. Bde., a letter was received from the OC 2/7th W. Yorks Regt. recommending him for immediate award.	
	27/3		Numerous enemy attacks beaten off, enemy pressure grew steadily less.	

Place	Date	Hour	Summary of Events and Information	Remarks and references to Appendices
ESSARTS	28/3		Bde HQ in ESSARTS heavily shelled - 3 huts hit - decided to move back to HANNESCAMPS - this was carried out in the evening. Lt W. CARDEW slightly wounded in the head at the time (remained at duty).	
HANNESCAMPS	29 30 31		Batteries improved their positions - arranged for dumps of 300 rds 18 Pr. & 200 rds 4.5 How. at gun line. Weather very changeable. Brigade about 3000 moved further to Rt. - evening South part of BUCQUOY village. Lt. C.W. ANDERSON takes over duties of Orderly Officer vice Lt. R. PENNEY posted to 15/1/90.	

Commanding 190th Bde RFA

WAR DIARY
INTELLIGENCE SUMMARY

190th Bde R.F.A.

Place	Date	Hour	Summary of Events and Information	Remarks and references to Appendices
HANNESCAMPS	1/4		Nothing to report beyond village of ESSARTS was intermittently shelled.	
	2/4		Lt Col. G.A. CARDEW returns to HQ DA HQ at SOUASTRE for two days rest. Brig. Genl. A.S.A. COTTON takes over command of group in his place. By a direct hit with a 5.9 on B/190's Men haros G. NEAME MC., Lt R. PENNEY, 2Lt V.F. VERSFELD were killed & 2Lt G.T. HODGSON was wounded. 1 OR killed & 6 ORs wounded. Captain W. HARRAGIN C/190 placed in command of B/190 pending return of Capt J.B. MILNE from leave.	
	3/4		Funeral of above mentioned Officers at British Cemetery BIENVILLERS 3 PM.	

WAR DIARY

INTELLIGENCE SUMMARY

190th. Bde R.F.A.

Army Form C. 2118

Place	Date	Hour	Summary of Events and Information	Remarks and references to Appendices
HANNESCAMPS	3/4	4 P.M.	On returning through ESSARTS from Bde O.P. Major J. O'CALLAGHAN M.C. R.F.A. C/190 was killed & a Sergt of his Battery wounded. Captain W. HARRAGIN wrote in a report of splendid behaviour of Lt. L.E. HUMPHREYS in shelling of B/190 yesterday, putting out blazing ammunition & restoring confidence in the men after the death of their Officers. Lt. L.E. HUMPHREYS recommended for Bar to M.C. already recommended for immediate award. Lt. A.E. CUNDALL to Lt. A.W. PEWTRESS temporarily sent up from 41 D.A.C. to B/190. Lt. L.E. HUMPHREYS placed in temporary command of C/190.	
	4/4		Brig. Genl. G.S. COTTON returns to 41 D.A. H.Q. Lt. Col. G.A. CARDEW returns to this Brigade.	

WAR DIARY
INTELLIGENCE SUMMARY

Army Form C. 2118

190th Bde R.F.A.

Place	Date	Hour	Summary of Events and Information	Remarks and references to Appendices
HANNESCAMPS	4/4		Funeral of Major J. O'CALLAGHAN M.C. R.F.A. O/190 at BIENVILLERS Cemetery at 3 P.M.	
	5/4		Very heavy shelling of all roads, villages, Battery positions from 5.30 am to 11.30 am with guns & Hows. of all calibres firing mostly gas. Enemy attacked & entered village of BUCQUOY. This Brigade covering front immediately to the N. & S. through village. S.O.S. lines to cover Counter attack by 42nd Divn. at a slow rate of two rounds gun searching on S O U T H of BUCQUOY, kept up. At 4 P.M. we were ordered to bring our lines in as our Infantry (63rd Bde) were withdrawing on the left to conform with the new line of the 42nd Division. Rest of the day & night passed quietly - we carried out usual harrassing fire on enemy's tracks & approaches. Lt. A. J. LAMB R.F.A. joined this Brigade for Reinforcement & took over charge of H.Q. Signal Section during the temporary absence of Lt. G. McHARG. Hospital in England	

Army Form C. 2118.

WAR DIARY
INTELLIGENCE SUMMARY.
(Erase heading not required.)

190th Bde RFA.

Place	Date	Hour	Summary of Events and Information	Remarks and references to Appendices
HANNESCAMPS	6/4		H.Q. & of this Bde moved into dugouts just E. of the HANNESCAMPS - MONCHY Road about 800 yds North of the former village. 2Lt. F.A. LAYTON, 2Lt R.J. BRIGGENSHAW } joined from Reinforcements. Three posted to B/190. Captain E.S. GRAY RFA. 187th Bde RFA posted to command C/190 vice Major J. O'CALLAGHAN MC. RFA killed in action 3.4.18. Shelling of Battery positions North of ESSARTS- HANNESCAMPS	
	7/4		Road by 5.9 Hows. Owing to bad weather there was only slight enemy shelling. Our shelling also deceased owing to poor visibility.	
	8/4			
	9/4		Gas shell concentration on LOUVIERE FARM. L18d at night	
	10/4		Practice Barrage carried out at 5am & 8am, on each	
	11/4		occasion lasting for 9 minutes. Batteries searching in their interior line.	
	12/4		Practice Barrage carried out at 6.15 & 8.15 am as for yesterday	

Army Form C. 2118.

WAR DIARY
of
INTELLIGENCE SUMMARY.
(Erase heading not required.)

190 Bde RFA

Place	Date	Hour	Summary of Events and Information	Remarks and references to Appendices
HANNESCAMPS	12/4		Considerable hostile shell ming of our roads & communications, weather conditions being good	
	13/4		HQ moved to the old German support line West of GOMMECOURT village, where they occupied deep dug-outs. Lt Col CARDEW was now in command of 3 Art. Bdes (190, 310, 311) covering the 125 & 126 Inf Bdes, 42 Divn. On this day we took over hour ground to the right — the necessary alteration of zones & registration of zones took place in a satisfactory manner. The enemy front now measured 2800 yds. On being informed that enemy trenches near ROSSIGNOL WOOD were full of troops — a concentration of fire took place at 7.40PM & later information went to hand that considerable casualties had been inflicted.	
	14/4		new Brigade O.P. named for the first time, near GOMMECOURT CEMETERY K5 a D.D. 1 Section D/190 moved forward to position L29 c 75.95 so as to be	

Army Form C. 2118.

WAR DIARY
or
INTELLIGENCE SUMMARY.

190 Bde RFA

(Erase heading not required.)

Instructions regarding War Diaries and Intelligence Summaries are contained in F. S. Regs., Part II. and the Staff Manual respectively. Title pages will be prepared in manuscript.

Place	Date	Hour	Summary of Events and Information	Remarks and references to Appendices
GOMMECOURT	14/4		able to reach enemy Batteries lines of approach etc near PUISIEUX. A/190 moved to position West of FONQUEVILLERS	
	15/4		2 Sections D/190 moved to position West of FONQUEVILLERS became silent. The principle of silent Batteries is to have 1 18Pr. Battery & 2 Section 4.5 How per Group disposed in depth to cover the withdrawal of the remainder of the Group the bank. The rear line of defence (ie the PURPLE LINE) at the same time. Positions to cover the PURPLE LINE were selected about this time - those for the 190 Bde were in L 30 a	
	16/4		3 Concentrations of fire on ROSSIGNOL WOOD & trenches near (with guns) during the late afternoon. Capt J.B. MILNE B/190 to be A/Major while commanding Capt E.S. BRAY D/190 to gun Battery.	

WAR DIARY or INTELLIGENCE SUMMARY.

190 Bde RFA   Army Form C. 2118.

Place	Date	Hour	Summary of Events and Information	Remarks and references to Appendices
GOMMECOURT	16/4		Capt. W. HARRAGIN C/190 transferred as Second in command B/190. T/Lt D. VYLE C/190 to be Second in command C/190 & to be A/Capt. No. 920057 Gnr. WORSFOLD J.W. B/190 awarded M.M. Immediate award. Date of act night 2/3 April 1918.	
	17/4		Lt. C.W. ANDERSON transferred to B/190 from HQ. Lt. J.E. HUMPHREYS do to HQ from A/190. Orderly Officers. 2/Lt. F.A. LAYTON reappointed	
	18/4		Major J.B. MILNE transferred from B/190 to A/190 has left 3 weeks at the Base after having been stale, has returned from his return from leave to U.K. C/190 moved to new position at E22d 2.8. B/190 do E22d 4.7 Provisional covering fire Barrage for raid on the Lucifer trench at K.II.b.9.2. by 5th & 6th S. Lancs. Battns. Raid was unsuccessful but	

Army Form C. 2118.

WAR DIARY
or
INTELLIGENCE SUMMARY.

(Erase heading not required.)

190th Bde RFA

Instructions regarding War Diaries and Intelligence Summaries are contained in F. S. Regs., Part II. and the Staff Manual respectively. Title pages will be prepared in manuscript.

Place	Date	Hour	Summary of Events and Information	Remarks and references to Appendices
COMMECOURT	19/4		Artillery fire reported to be accurate. Failure was due to enemy Machine guns bombers.	
	20/4		2/Lt. H.G. CARTER joined, posted to B/190.	
			2/Lt. F. DEVONALD do C/190	
			Lt. M. RONALD do D/190	
			Moved HQ. to Chateau de la HAIE (J.6.b.)	
	21/4 }			
	22/4 }			
	23/4 }		Nothing unusual to report.	
	24/4 }			
	25/4 }		Concentrations on approaches from PUISIEUX - enemy relief - result not known.	
	26/4		Very quiet day.	
	27/4		Lt. T. WALTER joined, posted to C/190	
			2/Lt. J.N. PURDON do B/190	

Army Form C. 2118.

WAR DIARY
INTELLIGENCE SUMMARY.
(Erase heading not required.)

190th Bde RFA

Place	Date	Hour	Summary of Events and Information	Remarks and references to Appendices
CH AU DE LA HAIE	28/4		Fired on enemy relief during the evening in concentration	
	29/4		Nothing to report.	
	30/4		Brigade handed over guns in position to 787 Bde, command of the Bgroup passed at the same time to Lt.Col. C. LYON 187 Bde. 190 Bde marched to PAS village for a short rest, coming at the same time under 57th Division in Corps Mobile Reserve. 2Lt. J. G. BUCHANON joined, posted to A/190. 2Lt. G. H. HALLAM do C/190.	
			Summary	
			During this period of action April 1st to 30th 1918 - Harassing fire on enemy approaches, trenches, billets etc took place each night. Gas was frequently fired by D/190 - a very large amount of ammunition was fired daily. The very arduous times are traced	

Army Form C. 2118.

WAR DIARY
or
INTELLIGENCE SUMMARY.   190 Bde RFA

(Erase heading not required.)

Place	Date	Hour	Summary of Events and Information	Remarks and references to Appendices
			In all ranks of the Brigade, who responded well to all the calls made upon them. Reinforcements, both of men & horses were continually received & the Bde at this date was only 78 OR's short & its lower mule strength.	

R Gordon Lt Col RFA.
Commanding 190 Bde RFA

Army Form C. 2118.

WAR DIARY
of
INTELLIGENCE SUMMARY.
(Erase heading not required.)

190 Bde RFA

Instructions regarding War Diaries and Intelligence Summaries are contained in F. S. Regs., Part II. and the Staff Manual respectively. Title pages will be prepared in manuscript.

Place	Date	Hour	Summary of Events and Information	Remarks and references to Appendices
PAS	1/5		Day spent in cleaning up together bivouac shelters etc built	
	2/5		All 4 Batteries are living in tents, bivouacs etc on the West end of PAS village - HQrs being in the village itself. Inspection of Batteries at 2.30 P.M. by C.R.A. 41. D.A. Weather improves.	
	3/5		Very hot thirsty day spent in cleaning up vehicles, harness etc	
	4/5		Nothing to report except usual cleaning up of horses painting of vehicles, gun drill etc.	
	5/5		2/Lt. R.J. BRIGGENSHAW sent to Hospital	
	6/5			
	7/5			
	8/5		2/Lt F.T. MOSS joined posted to A/190	
			2/Lt R.A.H. TURNER do do D/190	
	9/5		Order "Pretac Battle Position" received at 7.15 am Bde Cdr got into touch with G.O.C. 127 Inf. Bde visual communication was established with Battery position. D.A. & 127 Inf Bde S. of SOUASTRE. Bde went for a short March returned at 1. P.M.	

WAR DIARY

INTELLIGENCE SUMMARY

190 I Bde R.F.A.

Place	Date	Hour	Summary of Events and Information	Remarks and references to Appendices
PAS	9/5		Following NCOs and men were awarded the M.M. for gallantry in the field (immediate awards)	
			No. 201487 Sergt. HERSEY J. A/190	
			18454 T/Sergt BROCKELSBY G.B./190	
			1569 Corpl. CRISP J.T. C/190	
			12231 Sergt. WELSH G. Acte. att. D/190	
			22311 Sergt. McCARTHY H.E. D/190	
			36674 Dr. BEAUMONT G.G. D/190	
			3676 Gr. JARMAN A.H. D/190	
			249524 Sergt. GIBLETT T.H. att. H.Q.	
			15230 Spr. RODEN W. att. H.Q.	
	(8/5)		18ctio B/190 under Lt. L.H PHILLIPS report to C.R.A. 41 D.A. COUIN to antitank duties, went into action as a Mobile antitank section 2 mile East of CHATEAU DE LA HAIE.	
	10/5		(nothing to report.)	
	11/5			
	12/5		No. 117980 Gr. F.L. BATESON A/190 } awarded M.M. (immediate awards)	
			No. 107126 Dr. WOODS B/190 }	

WAR DIARY
INTELLIGENCE SUMMARY.

190th Bde RFA

Army Form C. 2118.

Place	Date	Hour	Summary of Events and Information	Remarks and references to Appendices
PAS	12/5		Section of B/190 under Lt. L.H. PHILLIPS was relieved by a section 285th Bde RFA returned to PAS.	
	13/5		Nothing to report.	
	14/5		Brigade entrained at DOULLENS en route for 2nd Army area, to rejoin 41st Division	
	15/5		Detrained at HEIDEBEEK station camped at LOVIE Aerodrome 1 Section marched to advanced wagon lines of 15th Bde R.H.A. east of VLAMERTINGHE & went into action N. of YPRES relieving 1 Section of 15th Bde R.H.A.	
	16/5		H.Q. & remainder of Brigade relieved remainder of 15th Bde R.H.A. Headquarters situated at REIGERSBURG Chau Sheet 28 H 6 c 5.55.	
H6c25.55	17/5 18/5 19/5		Registration was carried out - harassing fire at the rate of 100 rds per 18 pr & 50 rds per 4.5 How per 24 hrs. MAJOR E.T. BRAY c/190 & LT L.E. HUMPHREYS H2 both awarded M.C. 18.5.18	
	20/5		Captain D.G. DUFF RAMC (M.O. 190 Bde) awarded M.C.	

Army Form C. 2118.

WAR DIARY
or
INTELLIGENCE SUMMARY.
(Erase heading not required.)

190 Bde RFA

Place	Date	Hour	Summary of Events and Information	Remarks and references to Appendices
H6b25.55	20/5		In order to disperse the Divisional Artillery in depth a new position was selected for 4 guns of C/190 at B2g d 40.10, where they would remain silent. The other two guns being left in to continue the harassing fire. Present Battery positions are A/190. I7a 50.80 B/190 H6b 99.50 C/190 H6b 60.40 D/190 I7a 60.90 Bde OP at I3c 8.0. Liaison duties. An Officer is sent to Inf. Bde HQ. for 7 days at a time. An Officer is sent to each Sub. Battn. in the line (c) for period of 4 days each. A new Gunnl HQ is selected at H5a 05.85 + a partie sent then	

WAR DIARY
INTELLIGENCE SUMMARY

Army Form C. 2118.

190 Bde RFA

Place	Date	Hour	Summary of Events and Information	Remarks and references to Appendices
H6 b 25.55	20/5		to strengthen the farm which have accommodation	
	21/5		Bde gave Artillery support to 6th Division (on our right) who were carrying out a raid on 21/22 May 1918. Zero hour 12 midnight. Duration of fire 45 minutes. Harassing fire reduced to 75 rds/m 18 Pr. 40 rds/m 4.5 How in action. 300 18 Pr. + 250 4.5 How per gun dump maintained per gun.	
	22/5		Nothing to report.	
	23/5		Lt. I. F. HUMPHREYS H.2. awarded "Bar to M.C."	
	24/5		Nothing to report.	
	25/5		Gas Bombardment (D/190) in conjunction with Heavies	
	26/5		Gas bombardment repeated.	
	27/5		2Lt H.Q. CARTER B/190 went to hospital (gas). 23d May night DILLY FARM – 2 infant were provided by	

Army Form C. 2118.

WAR DIARY
INTELLIGENCE SUMMARY.
(Erase heading not required.)

190 Bde RFA

Instructions regarding War Diaries and Intelligence Summaries are contained in F. S. Regs., Part II. and the Staff Manual respectively. Title pages will be prepared in manuscript.

Place	Date	Hour	Summary of Events and Information	Remarks and references to Appendices
H.6625.55	27/5		thin cloud. Raid unsuccessful	
	28/5		Nothing to report.	
	29/5		Small raid on 115th Siema in enemy Post. Enemy in large numbers attacked our raiders – no identification obtained. Guns in the trench of 118 Pr Battery section of How. 187 Bde.	
	30/5		4 guns C/190 moved to new position (must move) at 11.45 PM. to assist our Infantry. Harrassing fire as usual. Heavy gas shelling (Mustard) of A/190 in evening. Immediate damage to the human swing to leather adjusent. Position temporarily evacuated.	
	31/5		Nothing to report beyond a further 16 men & 3 Officers of A/190 were sent down as a result of the gas shelling of the day before.	Officers were Major E Arenhold Aug. O/C. Lt R.B. Buchanan 2/Lt. F.T. M???

Commanding 190 Bde RFA.

Lt Colonel Commanding 190th Bde RFA.

Army Form C. 2118.

WAR DIARY
INTELLIGENCE SUMMARY.
(Erase heading not required)

190th Bde R.F.A

Place	Date	Hour	Summary of Events and Information	Remarks and references to Appendices
T.b. 3.5.	1/6		Unusually quiet day. Publication of MENTIONS (Birthday Honours Italy) Following officers then of this Bde were mentioned:— Lt.Col. G.A. CARDEW C.M.G. D.S.O. Major J. BARCLAY MILNE B/190. Major E.J. BRAY M.C. C/190 Captain D.G. DUFF Mc RAMC att. 190th Bde RFA No. 45124 Gr. J. KIRBY C/190. L.817 Sergt. C.H. BROWN C/190 45283 Gr. C. STEPNEY A/190 37046 Gr. (L/Bdr) ARMSTRONG D/190.	
	2/6		Orders received for the relief of 41st Division by 49th Division on Major E.J. Bray leave to U.K. (14 days). Shelling of Chateau REIGERSBURG Tgrounds with 4.2 Tgas shell.	
	3/6		HQ 190 Bde move to Farm at I 5 a 05 85 at 4 PM	

Army Form C. 2118.

WAR DIARY
INTELLIGENCE SUMMARY.
(Erase heading not required.)

190th Bde RFA

Place	Date	Hour	Summary of Events and Information	Remarks and references to Appendices
TSa05.85	3/6		Visit in afternoon by Officers of 246th Bde RFA who will relieve the Bde on 5th inst.	
	4/6		Quiet day. Relief of 1 Section per Battery completed in night.	
	5/6		Relief completed. Lt Bland A5 A/190 & Rev. O. DUDLEY CF RC attached 190 Bde RFA wounded by bombs at night in A/190 wagon line. 2 ORs killed 4 wounded also by the same bomb. 2Lt R.A.H. TURNER to hospital (Mustard gas poison)	
	6/6		Marched to BAMBECQUE area from wagon lines starting at 7 a.m. Lt L.E. HILLS A/190 to Hospital (sick). Lt B. MIDDLETON returned to D/190 from acting as O.O.	
	7/6		2/Lt R.S. BRIGGENSHAW from B/190 to Bde HQ as O.O. Marched to ZEGGER-CAPEL-ERINGHEM Lt Col. G.A. CARDEW & Major J.B. MILNE were sick with Influenza travelled by Ambulance	

Army Form C. 2118.

WAR DIARY
INTELLIGENCE SUMMARY.
(Erase heading not required.)

190th Bde RFA

Place	Date	Hour	Summary of Events and Information	Remarks and references to Appendices
ERINGHEM	8/6		Marched to MUNCQ NIEURLIET to rest billets at 8.30 am 1/Col G.A. CARDEW gMajor J.B. MILNE still sick. Brigade watched by G.O.C. 41st Division on WATTEN Hill en route	
	9/6		Battalion Honours published (Italy) as follows (London Gazette Supplement dated 3.6.18) MILITARY CROSS for Capt. W.A. MACKENZIE RFA Adjutant 190th Bde RFA Capt. D. VYLE RFA C/190 D.C.M. for 249525 Confl. REID A.H. Signal Section attd 190 Bde RFA M.S.M. for 47163 Sergt. PETTY H.A. B/190 44582 Confl. HANNINGTON A. A/190	
	10/6		Informal inspection of C gA Batteries by M.G. RA 2nd Army	

Army Form C. 2118.

WAR DIARY
or
INTELLIGENCE SUMMARY.

(Erase heading not required.)

190th Bde RFA

Instructions regarding War Diaries and Intelligence Summaries are contained in F.S. Regs., Part II. and the Staff Manual respectively. Title pages will be prepared in manuscript.

Place	Date	Hour	Summary of Events and Information	Remarks and references to Appendices
MUNCQ NIEURLET	11/6		Training of Brigade	
	12/6		At R.M. MARIANS A/190 & Hospital. Training continues.	
	13/6		Arrangements made for a demonstration Barrage in the training area for the edification of the American troops. 2Lt J.Q. Buchanan R.F.A A/190 rejoins from hospital.	
	14/6		Train	
	15/6		Epidemic of Influenza in C/190 – Battery rather short in consequence – sick men unfit to use train	
	16/6		Captain R.L. CREASY MC hated to be train G.K. JENKINS MC RFA vacated to England. Demonstration for American troops takes place South of CALAIS – SOMER Rd. Barrage lasts from 1 P.M. to 7.30 P.M. Canvas village much knocked about shooting – very good, about 50 rds p.g. fired in all.	
	17/6		2Lt G.A. CARDEW & Major J.B. MILNE go to Calais for two days Capt MACKENZIE in temporary command of B/190	

WAR DIARY
INTELLIGENCE SUMMARY.

Army Form C. 2118.

190th Bde RFA

Place	Date	Hour	Summary of Events and Information	Remarks and references to Appendices
MUNCQ NIEURLET	18/6		2/Lt P.R. LANGHORN att'd C/190 to Hospital	
	19/6		CRA inspects A & B Batteries coming into action with rein drill	
	20/6		Lt Col G.A. CARDEW & Major J.B. MILNE returned last night from CALAIS. Lt H. PARKER C/190 leave to U.K. 14 days	
	21/6		Lt H.G. MASON B/190 leave to U.K. 14 days. Bde Route march & Battery remain in billets owing to epidemic.	
	22/6		Inspection of A B & C Batteries by G.O.C. RA VII Corps. Training continues epidemic spreads to Bde HQ where 18 men are suffering from it.	
	23/6			
	24/6		Inspection of Bde in Drill Order by G.O.C. II nd Army in No. 2 Section 4th DAG's field at RUMMINGHEM — rain shook the turn out — but the turn out was good nevertheless. Lt C.W. ANDERSON RFA B/190 to hospital	
	25/6		Brigade marches to ERINGHEM area. Battery Orders go forward by lorry to see positions between ABEELE & POPERINGHE that we shall take over from the French	

WAR DIARY
or
INTELLIGENCE SUMMARY.
(Erase heading not required.)

Army Form C. 2118.

190th Bde R.F.A.

Place	Date	Hour	Summary of Events and Information	Remarks and references to Appendices
ERINGHEM	26/6		Col. Adjutant & 2 Officers per Bty. go up to take over from the French Reserve position viz. Luvina, MT. KEMMEL. Bde. marches in at dusk to reserve position.	
	27/6		Nothing to report.	
	28/6		Bde. Bty. Comdrs. meet CRA near RENINGHELST – ABEELE Rd. to see positions in the line occupied by French 7th Division whom we shall shortly relieve. Reconnoitre fresh positions TW. Lines.	
	29/6		1 Section per Bty. goes into action in the line.	
	30/6		1 Section per Bty. relieves 1 section 7th French Division. Batteries move to new W. lines near ABEELE. Captain R.L. CREASY MC D/190 to be Major. Lt. L.F. HILL RFA A/190 returned from Hospital.	

[signature] Lt. Col. RFA
Commanding 190th Bde R.F.A.

WAR DIARY
INTELLIGENCE SUMMARY.

Army Form C. 2118.

190 = Bde RFA

961 27

Place	Date	Hour	Summary of Events and Information	Remarks and references to Appendices
27/A.14.d.00.95	1/7		Bde HQ. moves up in evening to take over command of Left Auty Bde in line to HQ at 28/Q.33.a 85.05. Remaining Battn relieving last Section French Auty Bde Command of heavy forces at 3 am Position occupied as follows:— Registration of 3 one 4 guns 2 guns A/190 M.4.d.43.84. M.11.a.65.40. B/190 M.4.d.20.55 M.11.b.25.77. C/190 M.3.b.26.25W. M.5.b.64.41. D/190 M.4.a.35.20 M.12.a.60.98. Bde OP. at N.13.a.65.70 Bde comms left half of 41st D minimal front from N.13.d.75.28 to N.9.c.15.49 behind the 123rd Inf Bde front of the 123rd Inf Bde.
28/Q.33.a.85.05				

Army Form C. 2118.

WAR DIARY
or
INTELLIGENCE SUMMARY.
(Erase heading not required.)

190 - Bde R.F.A.

Place	Date	Hour	Summary of Events and Information	Remarks and references to Appendices
G.23.685.05	3/7		Policy adopted – to do no harassing or unnecessary firing until ordered by D.A. H.Q. on account of the large amount of work to be carried out in the forward area	
	4/7		Lt. C.W. ANDERSON B/190 returned from hospital to 2/Lt R.A.H TURNER D/190 do	
	5/7		Inspection of Batteries by G.O.C. 41st Division – huments.	
	6/7		Major E.BRANDISH M.C. A/190 rejoins from sick leave	
	7/7		Nothing to report – maximum of 100 rds /By Bde fired per 24 hrs	
	8/7		Capt. G.A.Mackenzie M.C. proceeded on leave to U.K. 2/Lt. R.J. Briggenshaw assumed duties of Adjutant.	
	9/7		Major E. Brandish M.C., R.F.A. assumed command of Brigade during absence of Lt.Col. E.A. Carter D.M.C., D.S.O., R.F.A. to C.R.A. Test S.O.S. with 122nd Left Brigade – night of 9th/10th – Time taken 19 mins 23 secs. Twenty knee also between line average received at Bde. H.Q. + amount of sleep.	
	10/7		Lieut. C.W.Anderson proceeded on leave to U.K.	

Army Form C. 2118.

WAR DIARY
or
INTELLIGENCE SUMMARY.
(Erase heading not required.)

Instructions regarding War Diaries and Intelligence Summaries are contained in F. S. Regs., Part II. and the Staff Manual respectively. Title pages will be prepared in manuscript.

Place	Date	Hour	Summary of Events and Information	Remarks and references to Appendices
G.33.d.15-60	11/7	–	2/L H.O. Nicholls reported for duty.	
	12/7		Test S.O.S. with 122nd I.B. Report very satisfactory – shell arriving within 3½ mins of time message sent from front line.	
	13/7	–	On night of 13/14. Party of 1 Off. +50 O.Rs. under personal supervision of 2/Lt. Col. E.A. Carter C.M.G., D.S.O. salved two 18pdr Q.F. guns & one wagon from position N.14.b.40.75.	
	14/7		D.A. Instructions No. 14 complied with for purpose of 6th Div. operation.	
	15/7		Test S.O.S. with 122nd I.B.	
	16/7		"dto" in accordance with instructions 41st Div. G.122/34/12.	
			122nd I.B. reports "S.O.S. left". Batteries opened but after investigation it appeared that enemy signal "Two red lights" had been mistaken for S.O.S. 122nd I.B. fnt reporting later that front was quiet. Time 2.45 a.m.	
	17/7		Letter received from Corps Cmdr. expressing appreciation of the work performed on night of 13/14 inst. Circulated to all Batteries.	
	18/7		41st D.A. Instruction 15 complied with for purpose of operation by 11th Queens. Operation successful – 3 prisoners taken.	
	19/7		During evening enemy carried out destructive shoot on C/190 position, causing no casualties, but destroying one gun completely, damaging a second & putting one temporarily out of action. Lt.Col. C.D.G. Lyon D.S.O., who was in position at	

Army Form C. 2118.

WAR DIARY
or
INTELLIGENCE SUMMARY.
(Erase heading not required.)

Instructions regarding War Diaries and Intelligence Summaries are contained in F.S. Regs., Part II. and the Staff Manual respectively. Title pages will be prepared in manuscript.

Place	Date	Hour	Summary of Events and Information	Remarks and references to Appendices
G 33 d 65.60	19/7		The time rendered great assistance in extinguishing the fires.	
		11.0 p.m.	New S.O.S. rocket Red - Green - Yellow fired for information thrown at G.33.c.5.5. Only one rocket successful - at 11.55 p.m. Two fired at 11.55 p.m. proving failure.	
		11.5. p.m.	Lt.Col. G A Carless. CMG, D.S.O, re-assumes command of Brigade vice Maj. B. Brandiel, M.C. who returns to command of A/190.	
	20/7	10 p.m. to 6 a.m.	Party of 6 officers + 40 O.Rs. under command of Brigade Commander relieved another 2-15 pdr Q.F. guns from position N.14.b.40-75	
	21/7		Maj. P.K. Creasy, M.C. to Div. Art. to take over duties of Brige Maj; Capt. E.O. Bryce, M.C. assumes command of 10/190. Group Cmdr. conference with C.R.A. with regard to scheme for special operation. R.C.S. of 190 Bde + B/150 reconnoitre positions.	
	22/7		Work commenced on the position in accordance with 41st D.A. Instruction nos. 997 and 998.	
	23/7		Capt. T.R. Milne C/190 on leave to U.K. Bremie D/190 "	
	24/7		A route raid carried out by 122nd Infty Brigade under cover of	

Army Form C. 2118.

WAR DIARY
or
INTELLIGENCE SUMMARY.
(Erase heading not required.)

Place	Date	Hour	Summary of Events and Information	Remarks and references to Appendices
G.33d. 65.60.	24/7	1.35 a.m.	18 pdr. Barrage from N14.b 56.00 to N14.d 05.-43., D/190 neutralizing T.M. Emplacements. Casualties few but 2 prisoners taken.	
	25/7		Capt. W.A. Mackay, M.C. R.F.A. returned from leave to U.K. & resumed duties of Adjutant.	
	26/7		Daily synchronised shoot ordered by CRA 1 Rd per Bty position to be fired. F.O.O. to shoot on result stunning. This day's shoot at 3.30 PM. 47989 Sergt. KIRKUM, J. B/190 } awarded M.M. (immediate award) 80352 Corpl GRANVILLE.F.A/190 } in connection with the salving of guns on the night 14/7 & 20/7. Harassing fire as usual — Synchronised shoot at 4 P.M.	
		12.15 am	Bombardment in conjunction with XIX th Corps Heavies, by Batteries of this Bde — D/190 } firing gas on certain target — 2 guns each of A & B/190 firing also with A.P.X.	
	27/7		Synchronised shoot at 4.15 PM.	
		12.30 am	Bombardment of Hedge N14.b 00.05 – N14.d 19.9, & Railway embankment from N14.b 33.33 to N14.d 15.87 by the Howitzers & a box barrage put round	

WAR DIARY
INTELLIGENCE SUMMARY

190 Bde RFA

Army Form C. 2118.

Place	Date	Hour	Summary of Events and Information	Remarks and references to Appendices
G.33.d.65.60	27/7		these points by 18 Pr. Battery to catch runners Turkish cavalier Result:- many Bosche seen to run away from these points, but no identification captured.	
	28/7		Nothing to report beyond usual firing synchronised shoot at 4.45 P.M. Positions being worked on (forward) by 66th D.A. Our own forward batteries being developed into 6 gun positions for hostile Offensive Operations. Ammunition being dumped at these forward positions.	
	(27)	12 noon	This Bde covers the 123 Inf. Bde (Outer Bde) only - 150 Bde AFA takes over responsibility for the left Bde 122nd Inf Bde.	
	29/7		Nothing to report synchronised shoot at 5.5 P.M.	
	30/7		Lt. L. H. PHILLIPS B/190 awarded M.C. (immediate award) in connection with the silencing of guns mentioned above. Synchronised shoot at 12.6 P.M. No more ammunition to be dumped at present. Heavy fire opened on Front line at 2.30am 30/31st. No Infantry action. Two Artillery Support called for - presumably an enemy attack on the Right of this Division - A/190 attached	

Army Form C. 2118.

WAR DIARY

INTELLIGENCE SUMMARY.

190 Bde RFA

(Erase heading not required.)

Place	Date	Hour	Summary of Events and Information	Remarks and references to Appendices
G33d65b0	30/7		to 11th A Bde RFA for tactical purposes at 9 P.M.	
	31/7		Nothing to report.	

W Jenkins Lt Col RFA

Commanding 190th Bde RFA

190th (Wimbledon) Brigade
Royal Field Artillery
No.
Date 2.8.18

41st Division "A".

Herewith War Diary for August 1918 of this Brigade.

[signature]
Major R.F.A.
Commanding 190th Bde R.F.A.

WAR DIARY / INTELLIGENCE SUMMARY

Army Form C. 2118.

190th Bde RFA

Vol 28

Place	Date	Hour	Summary of Events and Information	Remarks and references to Appendices
G33 b5.b.0	1/8		Ordinary harassing fire of 270 rds /B 18 Pr. Battery & 200 rds 4.5 How.	
	2/8		Nothing to report - rain started about 10.30 am & continued all day	
			Usual harassing fire	
	3/8		Arrangements discussed for small operation (about the Rt. of B/94) by 122 Inf Bde to take off a small salient for which Operation 330 of the Bde will send a sectn from main position to reinforce forward section B/190 will send a section from main position to reinforce forward section. 2/Lt H. PARKER & 2/Lt F DEVONALD & 190 wounded the M.C. & then return to battery their position was being heavily shelled.	
			Harassing fire thru day only reduced to one half normal expenditure	
			Enemy shelled forward area thru harassing with 8 inch. No damage to the Brigade.	
	4/8		Enemy's H.V. guns very active today on Battery areas shell stores 1 O R killed 11 wounded Headquarters at 3.15 PM Parade before Army Commander & Representatives of every Unit	

WAR DIARY or INTELLIGENCE SUMMARY.

Army Form C. 2118.

190th Bde RFA

Place	Date	Hour	Summary of Events and Information	Remarks and references to Appendices
G3d 65 60	5/8		Harassing fire now taken the form of wire cutting. General Bombardment of enemy's forward system. Garrison fire handed by this group for T.M.'s forms on vicinity of N19a 45.00 between 8 P.M. to 8.45 P.M.	
	6/8		Visit by H.M. the King to area - party of Officers & 12 men get to know the route. Lt. L.H. PHILLIPS B/190 proceeds on 14 days leave to U.K.	
	7/8		Quiet day - nothing to report. 1 section each of B & C/190 move up from rear to forward positions to take part in impending Operation.	
	8/8		Quiet day. Registration of guns from new positions. Garrison fire handed by group for Divisional T.M.s firing on area about N24d 4.4. from 8 P.M. to 8.30 P.M. At midnight 8/9 August 15th HANTS attack on a line from N14c 82.96 to N15a 87.65 covered by Divisional Arty. operations. Been complete success except for two small posts on extreme left - about 30 prisoners taken, several Bosche killed - at the same hour a small raid on the Rt of Divisional area by the R.W. 3rd Rds results in capture of one	

WAR DIARY

INTELLIGENCE SUMMARY.

Army Form C. 2118.

190 Bde RFA

Place	Date	Hour	Summary of Events and Information	Remarks and references to Appendices
Essd 6c 60	8/8		Harassing G.M.G. Enemy retaliation to a few guns of this Bde assisted in covering their operation. Enemy retaliation for both operations mainly fell on Front Line support line - a few on Battery area inclusive	
	9/8		Reinforcing guns return to old position quiet day & night	
	10/8		Lt Col. G.A. CARDEW CMG DSO goes to H2 41st Division to act as CRA during absence of that Officer on leave. Major E. BRANDISH MC RFA A/190 taken over Command of Bde in his absence. LT L. HILLS A/190 proceeds to U.K. on 14 days leave	
	11/8		Heavy bombardment of our Front Line without break at 3.10 am to 4 am. Lt H. PARKER MC C/190 wounded at the Bde O.P. Counter-preparation "B" ordered at 3.30am - 4.30am Battery reverting on their S.O.S. lines in bursts of two Enemy attacked about 4.15am. C/190 ordered to assist Left Group. Our fire was slow rate of fire in 30 S lines. The part affected was our new F.L.T. seized from the enemy on the 8th inst Counter preparation fired from 3.15am to 3.45am. No further enemy attack	
	12/8			

Army Form C. 2118.

WAR DIARY
or
INTELLIGENCE SUMMARY.
(Erase heading not required.)

190th - Bde RFA

Place	Date	Hour	Summary of Events and Information	Remarks and references to Appendices
G32 d 65.60.	12/8		Fairly quiet day. Lt. C.H. LOUGHNAN D/190 granted special leave to U.K. Enemy shells bw Heavies at 6.30 PM SW of RENINGHELST with 150 mm	
	13/8		Hour 30 rounds fell near Bde H.Q RS. Counter Preparation fired in bursts on left enemy Front between 3 am + 4 am to break up any further counter attack by the enemy. Quiet day. Very little retaliation except on forward areas for our short Counter Preparation fired between 3.15, 9.3.45 am. Some enemy shelling of Forward system on the left just before the Counter preparation was started.	
	14/8		No action followed. Enemy started shelling area about M.3.b at 7.30 am with reaction ended of 150 mm + 210 mm have at about 2 minute intervals - still shelling at noon. Shelling ceased at 4.30 PM - large dump of SA. TM ammunition blown up in M.3.d. 2 guns of C/190 slightly damaged in the whole but remain in action	
	15/8		Enemy started shelled same area as yesterday with 210 mm + 100 mm	

Army Form C. 2118.

WAR DIARY
or
INTELLIGENCE SUMMARY

190th Bde R.F.A.

(Erase heading not required.)

Place	Date	Hour	Summary of Events and Information	Remarks and references to Appendices
G 33d 65 60	15/8		8.30 am & 10 am Shelling from 2 - 2.15 PM. Quiet day otherwise. 91.90 moved from M3 C 20.60 & M3 B 80.75 (approx)	
	(14/8)		(All Batteries cooperated with Heavies in a road blocking shoot on roads converging at Kennel village for 5 minutes at 10.10 PM)	
	16/8		At request of Infantry Bde (123) S.O.S. was fired at 4.20am - 4.35 am this morning. Heavy shelling of our front, but no infantry attack followed. Orders received for the relief of Divisional Artillery by 66th D.A. Capt E.O. PRYCE MC. D/190 proceeded 10 days Horsemaster's Course R.S. D'ville?	
	17/8		9.40 shoot by Heavies & D/190 supported by forward section of Bde from 9.45 PM to 1.45 am 17/8 but was interrupted at 10.10 PM by the S.O.S. Rocket being sent up - all Batteries immediately fired on S.O.S. lines, till about 11.5 PM when situation reported normal again - enemy had been on attacked on our front, into which batteries divisional of 190 Bn short cancelled	
	17/8		Quiet day - forward section were relieved by 331st Bde R.F.A in daylight guns being exchanged.	
	18/8		Remainder of Bde @ HDRS relieved by 331st Bde. On relief Bde moved	

Army Form C. 2118.

WAR DIARY
INTELLIGENCE SUMMARY

190 Bde RFA

(Erase heading not required.)

Place	Date	Hour	Summary of Events and Information	Remarks and references to Appendices
27/K22a 9.7	18/8		to Wagon lines about 27/K22a with one section in Observation cooring & Pottersyle line. (2nd Position.)	
	19/8		Got settled into new W. Lines.	
	20/8		2/Lt. LANGHORN attached C/190 leave to U.K. 14 days. Capt. T.B. MILNE returned from leave 18/8/18 having had 25 days in all (2 extensions) Lt. T.E. WHEATE C/190 returned from leave 17/8/18. 2/Lt. F. DEVONALD Mr. C/190 returned from 2nd Army Art. School 16/8/18. Nothing to report.	
	21/8		Nothing to report.	
	22/8		Lt Col. G.A. CARDEW CMG. DSO. proceeds on 14 days leave to U.K. from D.A.H.Q. 2/Lt. H.W. NICHOLLS A/190 } Leave from Course Muckingham 22-27th inst. 2/Lt. N PURDON B/190 } Lt. T. WALTER C/190 }	
	23/8		2/Lt. G/H HALLAM C/190 XIII Corps Gas School Course 23/8/18 - 10/9/18. Major E.T. BRAY Mc C/190 B.C. Course Shoeburyness 25/8/18.	

WAR DIARY
INTELLIGENCE SUMMARY.

Army Form C. 2118.

190th Bde. RFA.

Place	Date	Hour	Summary of Events and Information	Remarks and references to Appendices
K 22 a 9.7	24/8		Nothing to report	
	25/8	11. A.M.	RONALD D/190 2nd Army Arty. School 25/8/18 – 21/9/18.	
	26/8		1 Section No Battery relieves 1/Section No Battery 331 Bde RFA in action in positions occupied prior to 19.8.18.	
	27/8		Remainder of Brigade relief completed. Quiet night.	
	28/8		Quiet day – normal harassing fire – 10 cm H.V. gun shells Reninghelst – Abeele Rd during evening. Causing casualties to Infantry marching up to the line.	
	29/8		34th Division Infantry start to relieve 41st Division – 101st Inf. Bde. relieving 123rd Inf. Bde. in the left sector. 41st Division quiet day.	
	30/8		Unofficial news that enemy is retiring on the front of next Division on our Right. Batteries warned to be prepared to occupy forward sectors positions	
	31/8		Enemy retires in front of us – Our Patrols reported on MT KEMMEL at 8 am. – Lt. T. WALTERS C/190 goes forward at 9.30 am with a telephone unit to maintain touch with Infantry	

Army Form C. 2118.

WAR DIARY
INTELLIGENCE SUMMARY.

190th Bde RFA.

(Erase heading not required.)

Instructions regarding War Diaries and Intelligence Summaries are contained in F. S. Regs., Part II. and the Staff Manual respectively. Title pages will be prepared in manuscript.

Place	Date	Hour	Summary of Events and Information	Remarks and references to Appendices
G33d65b0	31/8	11 am	4 guns C/190 advance to forward position - in action at 11.30 am. All advance wagon lines to be occupied forthwith remaining B atteries steadily advance positions with all guns by 2 PM. Battery Comdrs. reconnoitre fwd position in squares N14 a & b. Our advance no troops eastward instead of SE - Infantry hold the line of the KEMMEL - NEUVE EGLISE Rd between N22 a & 60.15 & N33 & 40. Protective Barrage arranged in advance of this. Guns to support front at 3.	

B. Bennett
Major RFA
Commanding, 190 Bde RFA.

Army Form C. 2118.

WAR DIARY
or
INTELLIGENCE SUMMARY.

(Erase heading not required.)

190th Bde RFA

V 8 29

Place	Date	Hour	Summary of Events and Information	Remarks and references to Appendices
G22d6560	1/9		Counter Preparation fired by the whole group from 3.30am - 4am on a line 1000 yds in advance of our Infantry. A B C Batteries reverty position in N14 a 16 with a section each by Sections so as to cover the further advance of our Infantry objectives when are as follows At 1st Objective N29 central - N23 central - N23 a 0.6. 2nd Objective N30 a 50.41 to road jctn at N30 & 40.74 - to Estates at N24 C 95.45 to N24 B 20.50	
M6c 3.4			Bde Headquarters moved to FROWSTY HOUSE at M6c 3 4 at 10 am 85th D/11 Batteries moved at 10.30 am to positions at N14 65.6 9 N14 6.7.6 respectively. A x C/190 moved to their forward section position at 1PM & D/190 at 3 PM 2.30 PM all 18 Pr Sections ranged forward for 30 mins. Just of a line between N23 & 24 & N29 & 30 D/11 flares & how on end of the battery mentioned above 2nd Objective reported taken by 7PM. 30S. Guns laid 300 yds in advance just right followed. D/11 successfully registered on Wytschaete by 7.00 in evening	

(A9175) Wt. W2358/P360 600,000 12/17 D.D.&.L. Sch. 52a. Forms/C2118/16

Army Form C. 2118.

WAR DIARY
INTELLIGENCE SUMMARY.
(Erase heading not required.)

190th Bde RFA

Place	Date	Hour	Summary of Events and Information	Remarks and references to Appendices
Mbe 3.4.	2/9		Party of 5 men per Battery start at 6 am under 2/Lt PURDON C/190 to make up the road East of Beauval Copse in N.15.a to so as to enable Batteries to advance later to positions in this area. Some targets fired on at the request of the infantry during the day to assist them in their advance.	
		3. 4.10 P.M.	on the front of the troops on our right flank our batteries continued harassing fire with 4.5 Hows. During the evening the two Infantry Bdes in the line viz 101 & 103 were relieved by the 102nd Bde. In consequence of which all the artillery covering this sector was formed into 1 Group made up from A/160 C/160 A.60 B/7 Bde RFA + this group formed 1 Sub Bde + known as Bde H2 moved to M.7.c.22. at 5 P.M.	
	3/9		Certain points which the enemy occupied were fired on by Batteries of this Group at intervals during the day.	
	4/9		New O.P. established at N.22.a.91.78 & the O.P. on Kennel Hill were given up. Waggon lines Oak Trench. Other hints on the edge of Lozenwood Hill	

WAR DIARY
INTELLIGENCE SUMMARY.

190th Bde RFA

Army Form C. 2118.

Place	Date	Hour	Summary of Events and Information	Remarks and references to Appendices
M 7c 2.2	4/9		were engaged during the day by Batteries. Enemy Batteries very quiet during the evening, presumed a partial withdrawal is taking place. Weather still fine but rather close.	
	5/9		Enemy Batteries quiet. 102nd Inf Bde comes into line at 8 PM. Takes over half Divisional front. Capt W HARRAGIN B/190 acts as Liaison Officer with 101 Inf Bde from 6.30 PM. Relief of 34th Divisional Arty by 41st in next sector to the left starts tonight A/190 relieving A/152 who come into the group in A/190's position. Lt Col G.A. CARDEW CMG. DSO. RFA. returns from leave to U.K. resumes command of this Group. Capt W.A. MACKENZIE MC. RFA awarded the Italian Silver medal for militan Valour (15.8.18) Concentration shoots on PETIT BOIS at HN 9.7 PM by D/11 C/190 285th Bty D/11 in in into Gnap Zone at 2.30 PM covered by 85 & Bty firing Shrapnel. B/190 exchanges with B/152 Owen during afternoon. Their position in DICKEBUSCH area. SOS ordered at 4.30 PM till 4.30 PM in consequence of	
	6/9			

WAR DIARY
INTELLIGENCE SUMMARY

Army Form C. 2118.

190th Bde R.F.A.

Place	Date	Hour	Summary of Events and Information	Remarks and references to Appendices
M7c22.	6/9		Heavy shelling of our forward zone	
	7/9		C 2D/190 exchange positions with C+D/152 during the day without incident. Capt. W.A. MACKENZIE (Adjutant) exchanges places with the Adjutant 152 Bde.	
H8c6.1.	8/9		Command of groups passed over at 10 am. Bde H.Q. established at H8c6.1. Battery positions as follows:— A/190 H22d 7.3. C/190 H28d 30.65. B/190 H29a 0.7. D/190 H28c 45.30.	
			Gas cloud attack. N12d8.8. to O1.b 30.15. Divisional front is held by 123 Inf. Bde with 2 Battns. in line + 2 in support (1 Batt. being lent them by 124 Inf. Bde.) This group covers the left Battalion. Bde O.P. Headly O.P. at H33d 3.3. is manned by Batteries in turn for 24 hours. Ammunition to be maintained at positions 500 rds per 18Pr. 400 rds per 4.5. How. Harassing fire carried out at night 125 rds per 18 Pr. Battery. 100 rds per D/190. Continued indications of a further withdrawal of opposite our front by the enemy, twice the prisoners statements, but it has not yet begun.	
	9/9 10/9		Nothing to report beyond ordinary Harassing fire. Weather very stormy.	

Army Form C. 2

WAR DIARY
or
INTELLIGENCE SUMMARY.
(Erase heading not required.)

190th Brigade R.F.A.

Instructions regarding War Diaries and Intelligence Summaries are contained in F. S. Regs., Part II. and the Staff Manual respectively. Title pages will be prepared in manuscript.

Place	Date	Hour	Summary of Events and Information	Remarks and references to Appendices
H8.c.6.1.	11/9		Steadily continuing shelling — only harassing fire to report.	
H.27.c.6.7.	12/9	10am	Brigade HQrs moved to WALKER FARM H.27.c.6.7. Weather unsettled – only harassing fire to report.	
			Capt. L.H. Mackenzie his R.A.A. gone to 4th A.R.M.B. for a month to learn the duties of Staff Captain.	
			Lieut. W.E. Williams his R.A.A. attached to Bde from 187th Bde R.F.A. taking over the duties of Adjutant during the absence of Capt. Mackenzie.	
			Nothing to report beyond harassing fire.	
	15/9 to 21/9		Nothing beyond harassing fire to report.	
	22/9	6pm	Bde comes under the orders of C.R.A. 41st Division. Bde covers Z24d42 to I32c23	
	23rd to 27th		Nothing of importance to record beyond ordinary harassing fire.	
	28th	5.30 to 6.15am	Bde turn barrage put the Bde covers in support of attacks by 14 Division. at 6.15am the Brigade reverted to the command of C.R.A. 41st Division. Orders were received at 6.30am from 41st Div to advance to position in area I24b.	

Army Form C. 2118.

WAR DIARY
or
INTELLIGENCE SUMMARY.
(Erase heading not required.)

190th Brigade R.F.A.

Place	Date	Hour	Summary of Events and Information	Remarks and references to Appendices
J.26.b.6.7	28th	6.45.	O.C. Brigade and Battery Commanders went forward to reconnoitre positions.	
		6.45.	Order to move from to Battery. Owing to the exceptionally bad conditions of roads and tracks great difficulty was experienced by the batteries in getting forward. However, R section of A.R.C. & B Batteries were in action by 11.5am and the completion however was reported at 2.30pm.	
		noon	Orders received from Bde. that the Brigade would support advance at 104th Inft. Bde at 2.30am. Brigade Headquarters were established at 40MG F.F.T.T.M.	
J.26.d.4.3		2pm	O.C. Brigade (Lt. Col. G.H. Gordon, Bde. R.H.A.R.A.) wounded slightly, but removed notwithstanding.	
		4.30p	O.C. Brigade and Battery Commanders went forward to reconnoitre positions in the vicinity of HOLLEBEKE CHATEAU (F.7.a.)	
		7pm	Orders issued from 49th D.A. to move forward and occupy the positions already reconnoitred at HOLLEBEKE CHATEAU. Batteries moved in the following order: D/190. B/190. A/190 & C/190. Again great difficulty was experienced in moving forward, owing to the congestion of roads & tracks. With the exception of C/190, all batteries reached their positions. C/190 had to drop into action at O.6.6. owing to the road forward being blocked. In leaving the corner of MIDDLESEX ROAD to go	

Army Form C. 2118.

WAR DIARY
or
INTELLIGENCE SUMMARY.
(Erase heading not required.)

Army Troops R.F.A.

Place	Date	Hour	Summary of Events and Information	Remarks and references to Appendices
	28th	6pm	Through BATTLE broke the leading howitzer of N/190 was slightly damaged by a bomb. Left sub section but probably accidentally on the road. It. J.B. BINNIE R.F.A. N/190 was wounded.	
	29th	12n	Brigade Headquarters moved to vicinity of O.6.b.	
		7.30am	Artillery support was given by Brigade to corps attacks of 14th Inf.Bde. the final objective of the Infantry the COMINES - YSERUS RAILWAY LINE from COMINES to P.29.c.9.0. was gained but not maintained. Enemy counter-attacked during the afternoon and gained a little ground, he was however watched later and at dusk the front line ran from COMINES along Railway to P.29.a.9.0. S.O.S. lines for the night were trench along the N. bank of the River Lys.	
		5pm	Bgde moved from O.6.b. to R.13.a.	
			Hostile artillery remained active throughout the day and night.	
	30th	1	The day passed quietly with the exception of occasional bursts of fire from hostile artillery.	
		4pm	Orders received from 41st A.D. that the Division would continue the march on MENIN on the 1st Oct.	

E.W. Warden. L.t.Col.
Comdg. 190th Bde R.F.A.

Army Form C. 2118.

WAR DIARY
INTELLIGENCE SUMMARY.
(Erase heading not required.)

190th Bugade R.F.A.

Vol 30

October 1916.

Place	Date	Hour	Summary of Events and Information	Remarks and references to Appendices
O.C.	1st	5.30am	The march on MENIN commenced. The Brigade moved forward to the 122nd Inf Bde. The Starting Point was Lane at TENBRIELEN CROSS ROADS T17a.00. Prior to joining the 122nd Inf Bde Column, the Brigade formed up in Column of Route facing South on the TOTDUOORDE - TENBRIELEN ROAD in the following order - C/190 HQrs 1918 D Battery. The section of C/190 under Lieut H. PARKER, MC RFA. joined the Column later at 6.50am. The remainder of the Brigade joined the Main Body at 7.30am. The remainder of Starting Point as the Road had been particularly heavy and devious. Notely Battery was active. Apparently was experienced by our side and devious. Notely Battery was active. It was reported that the Vanguard Commander had reached AMERICA without opposition. From the morning mist began to clear and the Column was seen by the enemy. Coming over the ridge immediately E of AMERICA and to at once opened a heavy and accurate fire [Artillery & Machine Gun] from the direction 800yds SE of WERVIC. The section of C/190 was to Parker at once went into action at Q.7a.87 and opened rapid fire succeeded in silencing the Machine Gun fire from about P19. Owing to the battle being but down on AMERICA CROSS ROADS, it was not possible to take guns into the exposed forward position. Orders were further	

WAR DIARY
or
INTELLIGENCE SUMMARY.
(Erase heading not required.)

Army Form C. 2118.

190th Brigade R.F.A.

Place	Date	Hour	Summary of Events and Information	Remarks and references to Appendices
	1st		Passed by O.C. Brigade for batteries to come into action along the Sunken Road about P.6.a. In order to the sunken road the batteries had to pass through a very heavy barrage at AMERICA CORNER. At midday the situation was as follows. Infantry took up a general line from Q3.c 37.6 Q8.6 central and the Brigade (190*ROH) in reserve in P6.a. The G.O.C. 130th Inf. Bde. decided that further advance was not possible without organized artillery support. Infantry Bde. HQrs were established at Q2.c76. Artillery Brigade HQrs were established at J36.d.o.o. during day. At night the O.C. Brigade and Adjutant went to Q7.a77 in order to be in closer liaison with Infantry Brigade H.Q. During the afternoon hostile artillery activity was mainly confined to "area shoots" & during the night to harassing fire over practically the whole Brigade area.	
J36.d.o.o.	2nd	3am.	O.C. Brigade sent to see G.O.C. 133rd Inf.Bde. in order to arrange the artillery support to be given to an attack which had been ordered by Division to take	

Army Form C. 2118.

WAR DIARY
or
INTELLIGENCE SUMMARY.
(Erase heading not required.)

190th Brigade R.F.A.

Place	Date	Hour	Summary of Events and Information	Remarks and references to Appendices
J36d00	2nd	—	Place at 7am. It was arranged that Batteries would fire as follows:—	
			18pdrs on line Q9b60, Q9b60, Q4c47. Howitzers on points between 18pdrs. This line was bombarded from 6.30 to 7am. At 7am the Infantry attack took place. The 18pdrs	
		7.45 to 8am	Batteries bombarded the following line Q17c9.0 — Q11a5.1, Q11b7.3. The objective was to secure the front and support trenches running S of the MENIN ROAD.	
			Known Kronge Square Q11b, Q17c r Q17b.	
		5.56…	The enemy counter-attack developed under heavy artillery fire of the situation	
		to	through the temporary success of the enemy became as follows:—	
		6.4 pm	Infantry of 89 civilian R10a 3.6. YPRES MENIN Road.	
			Infantry of the Division were relieved by 102nd Bde (34th Division).	
		(later)	O.C. Brigade Adjutant went up to vicinity of Q9a77 in order to be in closer touch with Infantry holding the line.	
			Batteries remained in action in 56a and HQrs at J36d00 by day and Q9a77 by night.	
			Hostile artillery and machine guns were very active during the day and increased during the night.	

Army Form C. 2118.

WAR DIARY
or
INTELLIGENCE SUMMARY.

(Erase heading not required.)

190th Brigade R.F.A.

Place	Date	Hour	Summary of Events and Information	Remarks and references to Appendices
T.30.c.c.	3rd		Batteries moved from Pop. to K.31.c. Enemy put down several hurricane bombardments during the day. Hygo men were ordered for after this arrival in new position of MADELIN and hammer and 5"H.O.men kicked of 7 wounded. Harassing fire was put down by batteries on area East of CHELUVELT – Chiefly along the MENIN ROAD as far as PRESND. Moch activity was this adren during night.	
	4th		Brigade relieved 17th Bde. R.F.A. + took over front Q.10 central to K.39 central from bars. Bde Headquarters were established at T.29.b.7.	
T.29.b.7.	5th		Brigade moved harassing fire. There is nothing of importance to record.	
	6th		Nothing of importance to report except usual harassing fire. 1 section of each Battery moved into position in K.32.b. + K.26.a. for the purpose of enfilading hun in K.35 + K.36. Harassing fire during day + night.	
	7th		Grand orders of Battery have registered on line in K.35 + K.36. by aeroplane and usual harassing fire. Harassing fire by day + night.	
	8th		Usual harassing + Harassing fire there is nothing of importance to record.	
	9th		Brigade usual shelling + Harassing fire there is nothing of importance to record.	

Army Form C. 2118.

WAR DIARY
or
INTELLIGENCE SUMMARY.
(Erase heading not required.)

190th Brigade R.N.

Place	Date	Hour	Summary of Events and Information	Remarks and references to Appendices
	10th		O.C. Bn. sent Ballin Commander meanwhile rode in from area	
			Went hunesending Harrowing fire, heavy mustard	
	11th		Hunesending Harrowing fire	
	12th		Hunesending Harrowing fire	
	13th		Hunesending Harrowing fire, Hunesending artillery of Battns were withdrawn	
			to their main Battery positions at 5.30 p.m.	
	14th	5.35	Brigade first barrage to new attack by 197th Division	
		7.5	Orders received from 4th DA by phone that Bn would advance to area of K30c	
		7.10	Orders passed to Battns. Brass of above:- A.B.C.B.	
		7.15	Batteries were clear of their positions + on their way to rendezvous at K28b, but	
			O.C. Bn + Battn Commander rode forward to reconnoitre positions	
			owing to heavy morning mist, much difficulty was experienced in	
			ascertaining the exact situation in front. Zero action of guns were	
	10.15a		in action at 9.45 and at 10.15 all Batteries were in action in area K30c	
K30c60.			Bn HQr were established at K30c60,40 at 10am.	6.77 Zero gun Battery
			in the K.1677 ———— was carrying a considerable amount of trouble	

WAR DIARY
or
INTELLIGENCE SUMMARY.
(Erase heading not required.)

Army Form C. 2118.

190th Brigade R.F.A.

Place	Date	Hour	Summary of Events and Information	Remarks and references to Appendices
	14th	6.30am	and practically holding up the advance of our own Infantry on the R.O.B. who were on our immediate right. The O.C. A/190 (Major E. Braddock A: C.R.A.) displayed great gallantry & initiation in going forward to a point any where up from where he could obtain a good view of the battery. He stayed there until 10.30am and by that had succeeded in silencing it. He & his men advanced after casualties had been caused to the crews. The battery was H. Bty, 80th FA Regt. II AB7G. was commanded by a Lieut d'RES. After silencing this Battery Major E/190 turned his guns on to some hostile machine guns which were causing trouble and successfully succeeded in silencing them. Other Batteries of the Brigade engaged machine guns S. of [illegible] and N.E. of the town.	
		3pm	O.C. B & C Batteries reconnoitred the whole of the front and reported the line as held at 3pm R2.a.9.0. along KROMBEKE to MATRON FARM — PARAGON FARM — ROSE HOUSE — PARAGON FARM — ADMIRAL FM — L.35.d.2.6. to CROSSROADS in L.36.a.	
		5pm	O.C. Brigade & Battery commanders rode forward to reconnoitre positions in L.34.b.	
		6pm	Following message received "GOC Division congratulates 190th Bde RFA on good work today especially A/190 in dealing with hostile battery."	

Army Form C. 2118.

WAR DIARY
or
INTELLIGENCE SUMMARY.
(Erase heading not required.)

90th Brigade R.F.A.

Instructions regarding War Diaries and Intelligence Summaries are contained in F. S. Regs., Part II. and the Staff Manual respectively. Title pages will be prepared in manuscript.

Place	Date	Hour	Summary of Events and Information	Remarks and references to Appendices
			Lt Corlert was wounded. 1 man killed & 1 wounded.	
		10pm	Message by phone from 41st DA to say No. 5 wire in our particularly to released on 15th	
	15th		The night passed very quietly — nothing of importance to record. Capt Flanagan left Brigade to command 87/89. Nothing of importance to record with reference to forward. 87/89 was withdrawn and	
		3pm	I/return to Blois. 87/89 came away under orders of O.C. 190th tie from the	
K26 a.95.03.	16th	6am	Responsibility for the front passed from 4th Division to 34th Division. Batteries were in K28 a & b.	It. Kaughnen
			withdrawn to Wörin in K28 a & b. H.Q.rs. was established at K26 a.95.03.	Ept to join 4/DAC on formation
			Orders received from 41st DA that Bde would march to MOORSEELE Area on 17th inst.	
			O.C. Brigade + Battery Commanders rode forward to reconnoitre new area.	
	17th	6.30am	March to MOORSEELE Area commenced. Order of march A.B.C.D. + H.Qrs. Starting point K29 d.o.o. ROUTE – K29 d.o. – GHELEWE – DADIZEELE ROAD – K24 a.5.4. K23 d. L.26.3.F.	
			MOORSEELE. H.Qrs. were established at L.17 a.5.3.	
L.17 a.8.3.			c/90 L.17.6.4.6. B/90 L.17 a.5.3.	
	18th		O.C. Brigade and Battery Commanders rode forward to reconnoitre positions	
			in H.13 + 14.	

WAR DIARY
or
INTELLIGENCE SUMMARY.
(Erase heading not required.)

Army Form C. 2118.

170th Brigade R.F.A.

Place	Date	Hour	Summary of Events and Information	Remarks and references to Appendices
	18th		Following promotions and appointments were sanctioned:- 2/Lieut (A/Captain) W. Harrigan RFA to command of A/167 Bde RFA 14.10.18. T/Lieut H.G. Moore RFA B/190 to be 2nd in command of B/190 & Harrigan 14.10.16. Lieut (A/Captain) D. Lyle C/190 to command of C/187 Bde RFA. — 5.10.18. Lieut E.A. Dunne M.C. RFA from B/167 to 2nd in Command of C/190 & Lyle 5.10.16.	
	19th		Nothing of importance to record.	
	20th		Brigade marched to HALLE via GULLEGHEM, BISSIGHEM — crossing R.LYS by pontoon Bridge at MSa 7090 — MARCKE and POTTLEBERG. Order of march:- B.C.D.A. Batteries & Tns. March commenced at 7am but owing to 35th Division being delayed, a halt was made at BISSEGHEM from 11.30 to 13.35. HALLE was reached at 15.15 hrs, and Batteries billetted for the night in N.2. Bde. H.Qrs. were established at N2 b.45.95.	
N2b.45.95.		10 p.	O.C. Bde. attended conference at 122nd Inf. Bde. H.Q., at which details of offensive advance on 21st & the artillery support to be given were discussed.	
	21st	7 a.m.	1 Section of A/B +C Batteries serious were attached to each of the attacking Battalions for close cooperation. The remaining guns of A/B +C Batteries and the 6 How. of B/190 went into action at	

Army Form C. 2118.

WAR DIARY
or
INTELLIGENCE SUMMARY.
(Erase heading not required.)

190th Bde R.F.A.

Place	Date	Hour	Summary of Events and Information	Remarks and references to Appendices
A34.c.S.S.			O7d & O8a. These positions were reconnoitred by O.C. Bde & Bty commanders at 5.15 am.	
		7.30am	Bde H.Qrs moved to M.34.c.S.S. & joined up with 122nd Inf Bde.	
		Noon	Owing to heavy machine gun fire from high ground in O17, O23 & O29, the advance was stopped in order that Artillery could bombard the ridge. The Infantry were to try and effect a crossing over the Canal under cover of the Artillery bombardment & form up on a general line O16/central, O22A.S.O., ready to continue resume the advance.	
O.I.C.9.4		6pm	Bde HQrs moved to O.I.C.9.4.	
			During the afternoon Major R.L. Creasy was badly wounded whilst reconnoitring the front.	
			S.O.S. twice sent fired on line O.29.c.6.0.40 — O.29.c.6.0.60.	
		10pm	O.C. Bde attended conference at 122nd Inf Bde H.Q. Details of Artillery support for the advance at 9am 22nd were discussed and it was arranged to put down a barrage commencing 9am line O.23.c.13 — O.18.c.4.5 and moving forward by lifts of 100 yards every 2 minutes until a line O.30.c.23. — Pigeonhut was reached.	
	22nd	11.34am	S.O.S. Signal from Cd the Battalion was answered by all Batteries.	
		7.50am	S.O.S. Signal from Inf Bde was answered by all Batteries.	
		9am	The barrage continued and batteries opened as arranged	

Army Form C. 2118.

WAR DIARY
or
INTELLIGENCE SUMMARY.
(Erase heading not required.)

190th Bde RFA (10)

Instructions regarding War Diaries and Intelligence Summaries are contained in F. S. Regs., Part II. and the Staff Manual respectively. Title pages will be prepared in manuscript.

Place	Date	Hour	Summary of Events and Information	Remarks and references to Appendices
	22.9	2.30p	O.C. Bttys attended conference at 122nd Inf Bde HQ. Details of Artillery support to be given for Advance of Infantry at 4.30pm were arranged.	
		4.25p	Barrage opened on line O22.d.0.6 – O27.a.0.6. O21.d.0.7. to Pozières. Infantry advance was to commence at 4.30pm.	
		7pm	Front Line reported as follows: – O22 central O23.a.1.9. O17.c.5.3. O17.a.2.8. S.O.S. Line was found 300 yards ahead of these points.	
		6.38p	122nd Inf Bde reported that Right Battalion had reached line O22.d.8.6. O23.a.1.7. O23.a.5.6. S.O.S. Lines were altered to conform with this change. It was officially reported that Major R.H. Creery had ROA during the morning on night of 22nd as a result of wounds received in action earlier in the day. The night passed very quietly.	
	23rd	9am	Front line reported to be as follows at 9am: – O22.6.44. O23.b.95. O17.c.6.1. along road from O17.c.55 to O18.a.1.3. Burst of fire of 10 minutes duration was put down over ground over which it was proposed to attack in 2 hours. O28 & O29 in order to search MG ground.	
	24th	2.15am	Battery fires Barrage on line O28.b.4.47. O23.d.3.7. O22.b.5.4. Road in O24.d. and O29.b. ½ O24 & O23 Ord	

WAR DIARY
or
INTELLIGENCE SUMMARY.
(Erase heading not required.)

Army Form C. 2118.

19th Bn R.W.F.

Place	Date	Hour	Summary of Events and Information	Remarks and references to Appendices
	24th		to carry attack by 123rd Inf Bde. Barrage was repeated at 3.30am & 4.10am but no	
			progress could be made owing to heavy hostile M.G. fire.	
		3pm	A.13 & C/ Batteries moved to positions at O.21.d.40.10 – O.21.b.25.00 & O.21.d.00.30 respectively	
		6/9pm	remained in action at O.15.c.15.45. E. Anson ROA B/190 was killed in action	
			just after his Battery had reached new position.	
			Barrage of "9am of 5 minutes duration was put down at 2.5.9 pm & 12 midnight 3am & 5am pm	
			on HOOGMOLEN VILLAGE, KIEBERG & KIEBERGMOLEN, KLIJTTE and Cross Roads at M.O.31.c.9.	
			was to search areas for hostile M.G. nests.	
			with the exception of usual M.G. fire and a few rounds from hostile Artillery on O.21	
			the night passed very quiet	
	25th	9am	Bde fired in Barrage to cover attack by 41st Division. Brigade Zone extended from O.22 central	
			to O.23.a.7.5. and moved forward by lifts of 100x every 2 minutes to line O.35.d.9.0. P.31.c.0.0.	
		10.30am	O.C Bde & Bty Commanders rode forward & selected positions in O.29a with a view	
			of covering final objective – L'ESCAUT between Y.9.d.0.0 & P.30 central.	
		6.40am	Batteries ordered to advance to new positions as follows: A.O.29.a.2.2. B.O.29.a.4.4.	
			C./190 O.29.a.6.7. D/190 O.29.a.5.9.	

Army Form C. 2118.

(2) 190 Bn KRI

WAR DIARY
or
INTELLIGENCE SUMMARY.
(Erase heading not required.)

Place	Date	Hour	Summary of Events and Information	Remarks and references to Appendices
	25th	11.30a	Battries reported in action.	
		3pm	Brigade H.Q. moved to O.22.a.90.40.	
		3.15	The village of DRIESCH (P.36.d) and road in P.36.c was shelled by Battery at the request of 123rd Inf. Bde.	
		7.30pm	SOS lines for the night were from 200x East of a line T.34.a.50.90 . Y.13.c.80.75. Harassing fire was carried out during the night.	
	26th	5am	Battries moved to new positions as follows:- A/190 O.35.6.60.45. B/190 O.35.6.60.70. C/190 O.29.d.80.00	
			B/190 O.29.d.47	
		11.20am	Infantry reached AYERGHEM and were pushing on to RUGGE.	
		5pm	Bde was relieved by 157th Bde RFA 35th Division and withdrew to area East of COURTRAI.	
			Bde H.Q. established at N.15.c.5.6. Lt Col Curley Bde G.O.50 RFA (O/C Bde) favoured bar to DSO.	
	27th	2pm	Bde H.Q. moved to N.D.6.3.9. The 13 Batt(?13) regiment Bde + was placed to B/190.	
	28th	—	The North Somerset Bde from 4th Division Trench mortars + was posted to B/190.	
	29th	Noon	O.R.A. 4th Division sent representatives of Arty Bdes at R.A.M.G. and attacks were given on position to support an attack by 35th Division on 3rd inst.	
			came going into action in P.31.b.7.c. and 3 guns of A.B.T.C. Bde + 4 MGs of B/190 went into action at dusk.	

WAR DIARY
or
INTELLIGENCE SUMMARY.

Army Form C. 2118.

190th Bde R.F.A.

Place	Date	Hour	Summary of Events and Information	Remarks and references to Appendices
	30th		Remainder of A.B.H. Battalion moved into action at Bugh.	
P25c3535		4pm	Bde HQrs moved to P25c 35.35	
	31st	5.25am	35th Division attacked. Brigade put down a smoke screen on area Q19c8.3 – Q14d.2.0.	
		8.0c41. Q26c15.	This area was also searched for hostile Guns.	
		9am	Report received that attack is going well.	
		10pm	Orders received from 44th Army Bde Brigade with reg'd Front between AVELGHEM CHURCH	
P25c3535			and P32 central from 5.30am November 1st.	

W James LtColRFA
Commdg 190th Brigade R.F.A.

Headquarters,
    41st. Division "A".

        Herewith War Diary for the month of December 1918.

                                Lieutenant Colonel, R.F.A.
2.1.19.   Commanding, 190th. Brigade, R.F.A.

Army Form C. 2118.

WAR DIARY
INTELLIGENCE SUMMARY.
(Erase heading not required.)

190th - Bde RFA.

VI 3

Place	Date	Hour	Summary of Events and Information	Remarks and references to Appendices
Sheet 4 1/100,000 4 K 23.78	1/12		Scheme for Army Education drawn up this month received & notified to the men	
	2/12		2nd Lt W. Wilson RFA A/190 appointed Bde Education Officer. Inspection of Batteries by G.O.C. 41st Division, who expressed himself very well pleased with the turn out & explained to the Officers of each Battery the outline of the Divisional Scheme for Recreation & Education through the Winter before demobilisation	
	3			
	4		Nothing to report beyond recreation etc carried out	
	5			
	6			
	7		Lt Col G. A. CARDEW CMG. DSO. returned from special leave to U.K. & resumed command of the Brigade	
	8		Nothing to report	
	9		do	
	10			
	11			

WAR DIARY
INTELLIGENCE SUMMARY

190th Bde R.F.A.

Army Form C. 2118.

(Erase heading not required.)

Place	Date	Hour	Summary of Events and Information	Remarks and references to Appendices
Sheet 4 TOURNAI 1/100,000 4K 23.78	12/12/18		Orders received for the march of this Brigade to the area N.E. of NAMUR to start on the 13th inst - weather very wet.	
	13/12/18		Brigade marched to TUBIZE arriving at 3 P.M.	
	14/12/18		do BRAINE-LE-CHATEAU arriving at 2.45 P.M.	
	15/12/18		One days rest in billets. a party goes in a lorry to see the points of historical interest at Waterloo - another lorry takes a party to Brussels for the day.	
	16/12/18		Brigade marches to BRAINE-L'ALLEUD - individual members go to view the Battlefield of Waterloo in the afternoon.	
	17/12/18		Brigade marches to SART-DAME-AVELINE	
	18/12/18		march continued to village of SPY - 7 miles West of Namur.	
	19/12/18		do BIERWAART & PONTILLAS	
	20/12/18		do HUCCORGNE & FUMAL	
	21/12/18		do VIEUX WALEFFE for Headquarters, the Batteries remaining	
	22/12/18		Lt H W NICHOLS A/190 rejoined from Hospital	

Army Form C. 2118.

WAR DIARY
or
INTELLIGENCE SUMMARY.
(Erase heading not required.)

190 Bde RFA.

Place	Date	Hour	Summary of Events and Information	Remarks and references to Appendices
VIEUX WALEFFE	23/12/18			
	24/12/18		Nothing to report.	
	25/12/18		19 men left the Bde for demobilization as Colliers	
	26/12/18		6 do do	
	27/12/18			
	28/12/18		Following Officers transferred to 41 DAC. Lt T. WALTERS C/190	
			2/Lt H.W. NICHOLS A/190	
			2/Lt E.A. REMNANT B/190	
			2/Lt J.E. HOPCRAFT D/190 (at present on leave)	
	29/12/18		Nothing to report	
	30/12/18			
	31/12/18		Following men left the Bde for Demobilisation	
			14 Coal miners	
			1 Pivotal man	
			1 Demobilisation	
			5 Wastage Details	

H. Parker Lt Col RFA
Commanding 190 Bde RFA.

Army Form C.

WAR DIARY

INTELLIGENCE SUMMARY
(Erase heading not required.)

190- Bde RFA

Instructions regarding War Diaries and Intelligence Summaries are contained in F. S. Regs., Part II. and the Staff Manual respectively. Title pages will be prepared in manuscript.

Place	Date	Hour	Summary of Events and Information	Remarks and references to Appendices
VIEUX WALEFFE	1/1/19		Nothing to report.	
E. not of LIEGE	2/1/19 3/1/19 4/1/19		Nothing to report	
	5/1/19		1 W.O., three next horse in a WATFORD DETAIL. 4 ORs sent home who have over two years of Colour Service to run. Orders received for the Division to start entraining for COLOGNE Bridgehead on the 6th.	
	6/1/19 7/1/19 8/1/19		Nothing to report	
	9/1/19 10/1/19		1 Punjabi man 2 Cool recruits 1 Demobolizer & Watford Detail proceeded to England Orders received for Bde to entrain at HUY to relieve 1st Canadian Division in the COLOGNE Bridgehead starting on the 13th inst.	
	11/1/19		Lt Col CARDEN proceeds to PARIS on 8 days leave - Lt Col MALLOCK temporarily taken over command in his absence	

WAR DIARY

INTELLIGENCE SUMMARY.   190th Bde RFA

(Erase heading not required.)

Army Form C. 2118.

Place	Date	Hour	Summary of Events and Information	Remarks and references to Appendices
	12/1/19		Nothing to report.	
	13/1/19		A & B Batteries entrained at HUY for Germany to relieve 1st Bde 1st Canadian Division	
	14/1/19		C & D do do do do	
	15/1/19		HQ 190 Bde do do	
	16/1/19		The Bde arrived at WAHN Barracks SE of COLOGNE.	
	17/1/19 to 27/1/19		Lt.Col A.M. MALLOCK returns to England to report to War Office. Major J.B. MILNE taken over command of Brigade. Nothing to report (20th - Lt.Col. G.A. CARDEW returns from Paris & takes over command of Brigade)	
	28/1/19		19 Other Ranks sent away for Demobilisation	
	29/1/19		7 do do Lt.Col G.A. CARDEW goes to HQ 41 D.A. to act as C.R.A. during the absence of Brig Gen A. Cotton on leave	
	30/1/19 31/1/19		Nothing to report.	

M Cardew Lt.Col RFA
Commanding 190 Bde RFA

Headquarters,

41st Division "A"

Herewith War Diary for the month of ~~January~~ February 1919.

28.2.1919.

[signature]
Major., R.F.A.
Commanding, 190th Brigade., R.F.A.

WAR DIARY

INTELLIGENCE SUMMARY.

190th — Bde RFA

Army Form C. 2118.

Month 3 4

(Erase heading not required.)

Place	Date	Hour	Summary of Events and Information	Remarks and references to Appendices
WAHN Barracks S.E. of COLOGNE	1/2		Lt. L. HILLS of Bde H.Q. & 9 other Ranks of the Brigade go off for demobilization.	
DEUTZ- COLOGNE	2/2		Bde moves from WAHN Barracks as follows:- Bde HQ to DEUTZ (No2 DEUTZ MULHEIMER STRASSE) A/190 to POLL C/190 do D/190 do B/190 to FORT IX near WESTHOVEN.	
	3/2		Nothing to report.	
	6/2		1 NCO + 5 OR 9th Brigade leave for demobilization.	
	7/2		Lt L E HUMPHREYS MC of A Battery assumes duties of Adjutant during absence of Capt. W.A. MACKENZIE on leave England. G.O.C. Division visits Batteries of the Brigade.	
	8/2		Nothing to report.	
	12/2		1 NCO + 4 ORs of the Bde. go off for demobilization.	
	13/2		1 NCO + 1 other rank leave for demobilization.	

Page 1

Page 2
Army Form C. 2118.

WAR DIARY or INTELLIGENCE SUMMARY

190th Bde. R.F.A.

(Erase heading not required.)

Place	Date	Hour	Summary of Events and Information	Remarks and references to Appendices
DEUTZ- Cologne	13th Feb.		Lt Col. MATLOCK returned having returned from leave to Bde. on 12th inst.	
	14th		M.G. R.A. & Capt. visited Headquarters of Bdes. in accordance with War Office instructions	
	"		Maj. E. Brandwick M.C. R.F.A. returned from leave & assumed command of Hd. Bde.	
	15th		Nothing to report.	
	"			
	20th		Two F.G.C.M's held at D/190 R.F.A.	2nd Lt. F. NASH D/[illegible] D/176 Row.8777 Gr. A.M. WILLIS N/[illegible] [illegible]/190 Ro. R.F.A.
	21st		Nothing to report	
	26/27th			
	28th		Battery positions to cover Trans. Loire of Livingstone were chosen on HOHKEPPEL AREA.	

Beaumont
R.J.A.
Cmmd.
190 Bde
Cmmd.

LONDON Division G.   London D.A.No.S350.
*********************   *************************

        The attached copy of War Diary of 190th. Bde. R.F.A. for
month of April, is forwarded to you please,

                                                          Brigadier General.
2-5-19   Commanding LONDON Divisional Artillery.

Army Form C. 2118.

APRIL 1919 WAR DIARY of 190th Brigade
INTELLIGENCE SUMMARY. R.F.A.

(Erase heading not required.)

Place	Date	Hour	Summary of Events and Information	Remarks and references to Appendices
COLOGNE	1/4/19		Advanced parties of DEUTZ a C and D Batmn Pole "B" Battery of OBERATH summary station and gunnery carried out by all batteries	
GERMANY	1/4/19		D/90. Calibration shoots. 21 rounds shell entry to Base	
	2/4/19		Lieut J.A.B. Wilson MC reported for duty and posted to D/40	
			Lieut Comr. B.A.H.Tranes posted to Brigade Headquarters as Intelligence Officer from D/190 R.F.A.	
	3/4/19		22 Reinforcements received from Base. Ordnance water carried to Ordnance rectifier carried out	
	4/4/19			
	5/4/19		One officer (2nd Lieutenant G.W.WILSON) and 11 O.R. sent to Constantinople Corps for engineers	
			34 L.D. animals received from Animal Corp.	
	6/4/19		18 R.A.O. received from Animal Corp.	
			1 Officer sent to the U.K. for Repatriation Captain C.A. DEWAR	
			Twohny {report}	
	7/4/19		Colonel G.A. CARDEN & two others sent home for R.A. Reform	
	8/4/19			

WAR DIARY Sheet 2
INTELLIGENCE SUMMARY
(Erase heading not required.)

Army Form C. 2118.

Place	Date	Hour	Summary of Events and Information	Remarks and references to Appendices
COLOGNE	8/4/19		One Officer (2nd Lieutenant J.W. Hood) and 19 O.R's sent to the Canadian Gunners Camp for dispersal	
GERMANY			Americans Army Colonels visited Head Quarters of this Brigade to study disarmament.	
	9/4/19		Return trip arranged by Division. 1 Officer 30 O.R's 57½ Jura	
			20 O.R's reinforcements received from Base	
	10/4/19		Lieutenant R.H. PEARS R.F.A. reported for duty in Brigade	
			Signal Officer	
			One Officer (Lieutenant L.H. PHILLIPS) and 7 O.R's dispersed	
	11/4/19		11 O.R's reinforcement received, otherwise nothing to report	
	12/4/19		Lieutenants A. REID and W.W. BORDASS joined for duty, posted to "D" and "B" Batteries respectively	
			One Officer (Lieutenant G. MIDDLETON) and 19 O.R's dispersed	
	13/4/19		131 O.R's Reinforcements received	
			Lieutenants J. L.A. NINCH reported for duty posted to 3 Battery	
	14/4/19		13 O.R's dispersed and 12 O.R's received as reinforcements	

Army Form C. 2118.

WAR DIARY Sheet 3.
or
INTELLIGENCE SUMMARY.

(Erase heading not required.)

Instructions regarding War Diaries and Intelligence Summaries are contained in F. S. Regs., Part II. and the Staff Manual respectively. Title pages will be prepared in manuscript.

Place	Date	Hour	Summary of Events and Information	Remarks and references to Appendices
COLOGNE	14/4/19		Major C.A.L. BROWN relinquished his duty and posted to "C" Battery	
GERMANY			Major K.P. ATKINSON M.C. assumed his duty and posted "A" Battery	
	15/4/19		Captain C.H. KILPATRICK assumed his duty and posted to "A" Battery	
	—		Lieutenant C. LAWLOR assumed his duty and posted to "B" Battery	
	—		Lieutenant C.A. SPARKES assumed his duty and posted to "B" Battery	
	16-4-19		Nothing to report.	
	16-4-19		Lieutenant Colonel A.F. THOMSON D.S.O., R.F.A. 156th relinquished command of the Brigade upon his return to Colonel G.A. GARDEN CMG 5th R.F.A. to the U.K.	
	17-4-19		4 Officers departed Lieutenants L. HUMPHREYS, A.M. RONALD 2nd Lieutenants R.J. MARSHALL, R.G. BROWN and 85 OR's	
	—		20 Men received from Divisional Rummal Camp.	
	18/4/19		25 OR's departed to Lancaster camp Cologne	
	—		Lieutenants L.A. WINCH and N.H. BURRALL returned on duty	
	—		Inspection of Horses went disposed of death	
	19-4-19		Three Officers reinforcements received	

WAR DIARY

Sheet 4.

Army Form C. 2118.

INTELLIGENCE SUMMARY.

(Erase heading not required.)

Place	Date	Hour	Summary of Events and Information	Remarks and references to Appendices
COLOGNE	19/4/19		Lieutenant R.T.J. PERRY-WARNES to C/190 Brigade R.F.A. 2nd Lieutenant E.K. DAVIES	
GERMANY			to B/190 Brigade R.F.A. Lieut. M.F.T. BAINES to D/190 Bde R.F.A.	
			36 O.R's dispatched to concentration camp COLOGNE	
	19/4/19		28 dratfees L.D. Horses to the Remount Camp	
	20/4/19		One Officer reinforcement joined for duty, Lieutenant M DUKE and	
	" "		posted to A/190 Brigade T.F.A. for duty	
			One R.A.V.C. Surgeon to concentration camp COLOGNE for disposal	
	22/4/19		Nothing to report. Ordinary routine and training carried on.	
	22/4/19		Nothing to report. Ordinary training carried on.	
	23/4/19		44 O.R's to Army Concentration Camp COLOGNE for dispersal	
	24/4/19		6 Bombardiers 30 Gunners and 22 Drivers reinforcements	
	" "		received and posted to Batteries for duty	
	25/4/19		63 O.R's received 1 Sergeant 32 Gunners 25 Drivers 5 Trumpeters	
	" "		and posted to Batteries for duty.	
	26/4/19		Nothing to report, inspection by C.R.A. London Division.	
			One Complete 18 pdr Battery and one complete 4.5 How. Bty	

WAR DIARY
INTELLIGENCE SUMMARY

Army Form C. 2118.

(Erase heading not required.)

Place	Date	Hour	Summary of Events and Information	Remarks and references to Appendices
COLOGNE GERMANY	26/4/1919		Inspection and re Solution in F.S.M.O.	
	27.4.19		Testing Draft	
	28.4.19		Training routine in the morning. Afternoon half holiday for Divisional Race Meeting.	
	29.4.19		Training and routine during the morning. Afternoon half holiday for Divisional Race Meeting.	
	30.4.19		Prepare parade for Commanding Ranks purposes of Battery relieved "B" Battery as picket Battery at DIERATH	

COLOGNE
30-4-1919

C.D. Thomas
Lt. Col, RFA
Comdg 190 Bde, RFA

Lt. Col, RFA
190 Bde, RFA

WAR DIARY of 190th Brigade R.F.A.
INTELLIGENCE SUMMARY
(Erase heading not required.)

Army Form C. 2118.

190 (Wimbledon) Brigade
No. 039
R. F. A.

Place	Date	Hour	Summary of Events and Information	Remarks and references to Appendices
COLOGNE GERMANY	1-5-19	—	Headquarters at DEUTZ. B, C and D Batteries at POLL. "A" Battery on outpost duty at OVERATH. Brigade Route March M.T.S.M.O. cancelled owing to bad weather. Inspection of horses by Staff Vet. Surgeon.	
	2.5.19	—	Revise and training. 43 Reinforcements received (2 Blm, 18 O.Rs), 1 Bdr, 14 Signallers, 1 Fitter, 25 gunners.) Posted to Batteries.	
	3-5-19	—	15 O.Rs sent to Concentration Camp COLOGNE for dispersal. 3 Officers discharged. Major J.B. Milne M.C., Captain E.O. Price M.C., and Lieut A.B. WILKINSON M.C. 1 Officer on leave transferred. Lieut M/J.N. Purdon.	
	4.5.19	—	27 Reinforcements received. 1 Sergeant and 26 gunners. Church Parade at 09.25. Afternoon half holiday.	
	5.5.19	—	Ordinary routine but special care and preparation for Inspection by G.O.C. in C. Army of the Rhine and Meuse Pass.	

Sheet 2

WAR DIARY
INTELLIGENCE SUMMARY
(Erase heading not required)

Army Form C. 2118.

Place	Date	Hour	Summary of Events and Information	Remarks and references to Appendices
COLOGNE	6.5.19		Inspection by G.O.C. 2nd Army of the Rhine and Mart	
GERMANY		1.15	Post Divisional Parade	
	7.5.19	10.15	68 O.Rs for demobilization sent to Dispersal Camp Cologne	
			Lt BJS ROPER C/140 Brigade RFA posted to SOUTHERN DIVISIONAL ARTILLERY	
	8.5.19		Lt. T.E.WHEATE C/140 Brigade RFA to UK for appointment with Command Paymaster CHESTER	
	9.5.19		An officer charge's down to held AFTERNOON DSO RFA Ordinary writtens and Summary	
	10.5.19		Inspection of new Billets and Stables offered Rue CAVALRY BARRACKS, COLN - DEUTZ. Afternoon half holiday	
	11.5.19		Church Parade in the morning half holiday in the afternoon Bombarders and Signallers received	
	12.5.19		Capt (A/Major) H BARTER BSO RFA reported for duty posted to B/140 Brigade RFA	
			Corps ADVS inspected horses of the Brigade	

Sheet 3

WAR DIARY
or
INTELLIGENCE SUMMARY

Army Form C. 2118.

Place	Date	Hour	Summary of Events and Information	Remarks and references to Appendices
COLOGNE	13.5.19		Lt. Colonel A.F. THOMSON DSO, RFA, assumes Temporary command	
DEUTZ	—		of the CRA in leave, acts as CRA.	
GERMANY			do	
			do	
	14.5.19		C/190 Brigade RFA received at 16 Brigade RFA as	
			Artifices Battery. JM OVERATH.	
			2 OR Reinforcements. Longevailly and Ixtel.	
	15.5.19		8 OR Reinforcements. 4 gunners, 2 Y.Brutcetmen and 1	
			farrier.	
	16.5.19		12 OR to dispersal Camp COLOGNE and 1 Officer (Lieutenant)	
			J. WILSON) MARSHAL FOCH visited COLOGNE. All units of	
	—		190 Bde. RFA lined the banks of the Rhine RHINE to cheer	
	—		him on his journey down The water.	
	17.5.19		2nd Lieut. D. LUMLEY reported for duty, posted to HQ as	
			Brigade Commander Orderly Officer. 31 OR reinforcements	
	—		received.	

Sheet 4

Army Form C. 2118.

WAR DIARY
INTELLIGENCE SUMMARY.
(Erase heading not required.)

Instructions regarding War Diaries and Intelligence Summaries are contained in F. S. Regs., Part II. and the Staff Manual respectively. Title pages will be prepared in manuscript.

Place	Date	Hour	Summary of Events and Information	Remarks and references to Appendices
COLOGNE DEUTZ GERMANY	18/5/19		Half holiday in the afternoon. Sunday.	
	19.5.19.		Ordinary routine and training carried out. Corps Commander visited STRATH and district.	
	20.5.19		32 O.R. Reinforcements received & posted to Batteries	
	21.5.19		Leave for Officers temporarily cancelled. Off' moved	
	22.5.19		Ordinary [?] and training carried out. Relay range practice [?] out on the banks of the Rhine above Germany.	
	23.5.19		4 O.R's to 5th Lincolnshire Corps Wagon [?] for dispersal	
	24.5.19		Ordinary routine & inspections in morning. Half holiday in the afternoon.	
	25.5.19		Church Parades and stables only.	
	26.5.19		Ordinary routine and training. Lt. Col. A.F. Thomson D.S.O. R.F.A. on return from leave of the C.R.A., relinquished command of the Divisional Artillery.	
	27.5.19		Ordinary routine and training.	

Army Form C. 2118.

5th Sheet
WAR DIARY
or
INTELLIGENCE SUMMARY.
(Erase heading not required.)

Place	Date	Hour	Summary of Events and Information	Remarks and references to Appendices
COLOGNE	28.5.19		Ordinary routine and training. 1 OR reinforcement joined.	
DEUTZ	29.5.19		as	
"	30.5.19		" 4 Drivers reinforcement joined	
"	31.5.19		Divisional mounted inspection carried out. 9 OR reinforcements joined for duty. Officers Rode in Farmer Cooker Barracks DEUTZ. Stay lying on the afternoon. C Battery 90 Brigade RFA had sports at OPLADEN.	
			Was during manoeuvres have been commenced in/Battery. Officers Rides have each Saturday morning.	

31/5/19.9

R.J. Irwin
Major RFA
Comdg 90 Bde RFA

Army Form C. 2118.

WAR DIARY
or
INTELLIGENCE SUMMARY.
(Erase heading not required.)

WAR DIARY of 190th Brigade R.F.A.

Instructions regarding War Diaries and Intelligence Summaries are contained in F. S. Regs., Part II. and the Staff Manual respectively. Title pages will be prepared in manuscript.

Place	Date	Hour	Summary of Events and Information	Remarks and references to Appendices
COLOGNE	1-6-19		Headquarters at DEUTZ, B & one D Batteries at POLL, C Battery at OVERATH. Church Parade in the morning, holiday in the afternoon	
DEUTZ Germany	2-6-19		Ordinary routine and training carried out. 60 Lieutenants joined the Brigade to be trained as R.A. Officers	
	3-6-19		Royal Salute of 21 guns fired on occasion of His Majesty the King's Birthday, 6 guns in action in East Bank of the RHINE across the River due north	
	4-6-19		Inspection of Outpost Battery ("C" Battery) by Corps Commander at 11.15 h. Ordinary routine and training remainder of Brigade 18.00 received as a Reinforcement also tanks and I Sherwood Smith	
	5-6-19		Ordinary routine and Training / Preparation for Corps Commander's inspection on 6th June 1919	
	6-6-19		41 mules and 6 mules drawn to Brigade. Ordinary routine and training	
	7-6-19		Officers made and inspections in the morning. Half holiday in the afternoon	

Sheet 2

WAR DIARY
INTELLIGENCE SUMMARY
(Erase heading not required.)

Army Form C. 2118.

Place	Date	Hour	Summary of Events and Information	Remarks and references to Appendices
COLOGNE	7-6-19	afternoon	Lt R.J. PERRY-WARNES to have Established Restrnts. (AS63/4 (O.2.))	Signed by J. Ritchie
DEUTZ	8-6-19		Establishments to have domicile for all dependants that apply — no otherwise.	
	9-6-19		25 J=40 RDCRAFT to have Establishd Authy (AS514 (O.2.)) Estab Apply of the Rhine Bank Nation, no Yearney ordus no Yearney orders June GOC in C	
			British Army of the Rhine	
	10-6-19		Inspection and Guard Post for later Commands in the East	
			hours of the Rhine — Lyceus of Berck prepared & have altered	
	11-6-19		Drawing routine and Yearney carried on. 3 Bdn received as reinforcements	
	12-6-19		Ordinary routine and Yearney carried on.	
	13-6-19		Ations routine and Yearney carried on. Lt/S/Lt Hg MASON & Lieut BLACKHURST (O.2.)	Authy AS5/4
	14-6-19		Two officers rode here. Annual inspection carried out. Officers and clerks attended lecture by Command Paymaster on Pay Issues Bnks.	
	15-6-19		Church Parades in morning, half holiday in afternoon.	
	16-6-19		Ordinary routine and Yearney carried on.	
	17-6-19		Orders to stand by for more forward movement in event of German not signing Peace Terms being hence 3-3 days. Outpost Battery	
			C/190 B/A rehieved by D/87 Bde B/A C/190 R/FA moved	

WAR DIARY
INTELLIGENCE SUMMARY
(Erase heading not required.)

Army Form C. 2118.

Place	Date	Hour	Summary of Events and Information	Remarks and references to Appendices
Cologne	17-6-19		190 Res. B.T.M. applied to 1st London Inf. Bde. into lieu Beaufort.	
DEUTZ	18-6-19		J-2 days. Preparation for move.	
	19-6-19		J-1 day. Dutch lorries of Bde. for which no train accommodation allotted, move with baggage wagon route No 2 by Dural Topi.	
	"		to OVERATH. Arrangements made for moving of Brigade Spare Kit and stores in Brigade Dumps until ready into Y.F. area.	
	20-6-19		J day. Standing by for orders to advance into Enemy Territory.	
	24-6-19		No further owing to Tactical Strike service negotiations carried out in the Brigade. The orders received with money.	
	22.6.19		Church parade afternoon. & half holiday. No orders received to advance. R.S.M. joined the Brigade posted to Rfts.	
	23.6.19		Ordinary routine and training carried out. No orders received to advance.	
	24.6.19		do	
	25.6.19		Ordinary routine and training. Lt. Ash at Thomas Sto. 14 days leave to U.R.	
	"		G.D. Dunlop to 4 days special leave B.U.R. No orders to move forward.	
	26.6.19		Ordinary routine and training. Lt (A/Capt.) D.W.H.Nd. to have Gibraltar around	

Sheet 4.

Army Form C. 2118.

WAR DIARY
INTELLIGENCE SUMMARY.
(Erase heading not required.)

Instructions regarding War Diaries and Intelligence Summaries are contained in F. S. Regs., Part II. and the Staff Manual respectively. Title pages will be prepared in manuscript.

Place	Date	Hour	Summary of Events and Information	Remarks and references to Appendices
COLOGNE DEUTZ Germany	27.6.19		Ordinary routine training carried out. Divisional Commander visited "A", "B" & "D" Batteries St POLL. Orders received for the Brigade to find a Salute 101 guns on the occasion of PEACE being signed. Firing Point at COLOGNE on West River Bank north of HOHEN ZOLLERN BRIDGE. Firing one Round over the River Rhine into GERMANY. 12 - 18 pdr guns in action. No orders to move forward.	
	28.6.19		Guns in action by 12.00 hrs. Inspected by Divisional Commander and Divisional CRA. Orders received at 17.05 hrs by 1st Army and direct from G.H.Q. British Army of the Rhine, that the Salute of 101 guns would be fired at 18.00 hrs. "PEACE SALUTE" fired at 18.00 hrs. Salute fired at 18.25 hrs 15 seconds. Church parades all denominations during morning. Half holiday in the afternoon. Orders received to resume NORMAL conditions.	
	29.6.19			
	30.6.19		Ordinary routine and training. A new "C" Battery inspected by G.O.C. Lower Division and the CRA.	

COLOGNE DEUTZ
30 - 6 - 1919

Ivor [signature]
Captain
Comdg 190th Bde RFA

WAR DIARY of 190th Bde R.F.A.

INTELLIGENCE SUMMARY

Army Form C. 2118.

Place	Date	Hour	Summary of Events and Information	Remarks and references to Appendices
COLOGNE	1-7-19		A, B and "C" Batteries of Poll & "B" Battery of OSTHEIM Keeps at	
DEUTZ	2.7.19		DEUTZ ferry ordinary routine and training	
			2 Lt T.E. LEVI gives to Brigade posted to A/190 R.F.A. ordinary routine and training	
	3.7.19		C/190 Bde R.F.A. relieved C/187 Bde R.F.A. at OSGRATH. The whole day given as a holiday to go to Brigade sports of the Rhine	
	4.7.19		Troops by order G.O.C. in C Brigade Army of the Rhine Major C.E.G. WOOLLCOMBE — ADAMS given the Brigade posted to command C/190 Bde R.F.A.	
	5.7.19		Horse Ride in the morning. Horse Saturday inspection by batteries. Half holiday in the afternoon.	
	6.7.19		Church parades all denominations. Half holiday in afternoon	
	7.7.19		190 Bde R.F.A. went to a special Tactical Parade ft to CRA. in the morning. B and D Batteries also manoeuvred for the British army of the Rhine Cinema a photograph	
	8.7.19			

Army Form C. 2118.

WAR DIARY
or
INTELLIGENCE SUMMARY.
(Erase heading not required.)

Place	Date	Hour	Summary of Events and Information	Remarks and references to Appendices
	9-7-19		Inspection of Batteries by G.O.C. Division	
	10-7-19		C.R.A. inspected H.Q.S. Batteries at 9-30 & 10.15. Speeches on Rhine Bank.	
	11-7-19		Training was carried out by Batteries	
	12-7-19		in the mornings till 12.30	
	13-7-19			
	14-7-19		Elementary tests for trades mts. for Cavalry Artillery 39th RFA Stores 17/1/19 Test also Battery paraded as a unit. Afternoon sports again in Afternoon before gunners paraded again in afternoon — Excursion for Plate Mark Funeral to Namal at Excertis D/155 R.A. attended	
	15-7-19		H190 weaker wounded before H115 R.A. attended	
	16-7-19		ball knocked but	
	19-7-19		Lieut Cann Inspection by C.R.A. H190 numbers	
	20-7-19		Training & No troop numbers E	

WAR DIARY
or
INTELLIGENCE SUMMARY.
(Erase heading not required.)

Army Form C. 2118.

Place	Date	Hour	Summary of Events and Information	Remarks and references to Appendices
#	20.7.19		Sports at Poll Mynyke given by NRA	
	21.7.19		Lt Col H.W. Thorn late SSO returned from leave	
	22.7.19		Cricket match between BA & North Gun Sch at Mynley Wood	
	24.7.19		Captain J.L. Newton from leave. Ordinary routine training.	
	25.7.19		38 Horses cast. "E" wounded. Eliminating trials for Gun Teams and fun. E Battery won for the Bde.	
	26.7.19		No Offence rides. Horse Saturday morning inspection less Divisional Artillery training. Eight Lockers Annual Horse Show sports by C/90 Bde R.F.A.	
	27.7.19		School parades for all denominations. Stables & remainder of day as a Holiday.	
	28.7.19		Ordinary routine and Swimming carried out	
	29.7.19		do	
	30.7.19		do	
	31.7.19		do	

31.7.1919

[signature]
Comdg 190 Bde R.F.A

Army Form C. 2118.

WAR DIARY
INTELLIGENCE SUMMARY
(Erase heading not required.)

of 190th Brigade R.F.A.

Instructions regarding War Diaries and Intelligence Summaries are contained in F.S. Regs., Part II. and the Staff Manual respectively. Title pages will be prepared in manuscript.

Place	Date	Hour	Summary of Events and Information	Remarks and references to Appendices
COLOGNE	1-8-19		Headquarters at DEUTZ, A, B and D Batteries at DEUTZ and	
DEUTZ	do		C Battery at OVERATH Germany. Drumhead Service	
Germany	do		eliminating orders for Army Horse Show to be run	
	do		and from worn by C Battery 190 Bde R.F.A.	
	2-8-19		Officers ride held. Usual Saturday morning inspection held.	
	3-8-19		Church Parade in morning. Half holiday in afternoon.	
	4-8-19		Whole day given as a holiday by order of G.O.C. in C.	
	5-8-19		Demonstration at Linden D.A. School by No 6, making grenades.	
	do		Football XI.	
	6-8-19		Ordinary routine and training	
	7-8-19		do	
	8-8-19		do	
	9-8-19		Officers ride cancelled, unspecified Officers Inspection	
	do		carried out. Afternoon as a holiday.	
	10-8-19		Church parade of all denominations	
	11-8-19		Ordinary routine and training	

WAR DIARY of 190th Bde. R.F.A.

INTELLIGENCE SUMMARY.

(Erase heading not required.)

Army Form C. 2118.

Instructions regarding War Diaries and Intelligence Summaries are contained in F. S. Regs., Part II. and the Staff Manual respectively. Title pages will be prepared in manuscript.

Place	Date	Hour	Summary of Events and Information	Remarks and references to Appendices
COLOGNE	12.8.19		Ordinary routine & training	
DEUTZ	13.8.19		do	
	14.8.19		Half holiday in afternoon	
	15.8.19		do	
	16.8.19		C.R.A. inspected "C" Battery STOPFEATS	
			Three inspection carried out. Orders received to fire salute	
			at 8.19 am on night of Army Council to COLOGNE on 17.8.19	
	17.8.19		Check parades for Salute demonstration	
	do		Salute fired of 19 rounds for arrival of Army Council to COLOGNE	
			Firing Battery "B" Bank of River Rhine nearly HOHENZOLLERN	
			BRIDGE facing due East. Fired by 190th Battery commanded	
			Major R. PARKINSON, M.C. R.F.A.	
	18.8.19		Ordinary routine and training. Army three above to	
	do		afternoon. "C" Battery took Roll Corps for Best R.F.A.	
			fun team	
	19.8.19		Ordinary routine & training. Army three show last day	
	20.8.19		do	

WAR DIARY
INTELLIGENCE SUMMARY.
(Erase heading not required.)

of 190th Bde R.F.A.

Army Form C. 2118.

Instructions regarding War Diaries and Intelligence Summaries are contained in F. S. Regs., Part II. and the Staff Manual respectively. Title pages will be prepared in manuscript.

Place	Date	Hour	Summary of Events and Information	Remarks and references to Appendices
COLOGNE	21.8.19		Ordinary routine and training	
DEUTZ	22.8.19		" Major K.P. afternoon M.O. & V.P.	
Germany	"		for Conducts Bakery Comrades Cave.	
	23.8.19		Usual inspection carried out. Afternoon ½ holiday	
	24.8.19		Church Parade for all units and ammunition	
	25.8.19		Ordinary routine and training	
	26.8.19		" do	
	27.8.19		" do	Half holiday in afternoon
	28.8.19		" do	Prize-giving Parade for Brigade
	29.8.19		" do	
	30.8.19		" do	Half Holiday in afternoon
	31.8.19		Church Parade for all denominations. Half holiday	
	"		afternoon	

Lieutenant M. Hyde
Comdg 190 Bde R.F.A.

WAR DIARY
or
INTELLIGENCE SUMMARY

(Erase heading not required.)

190th Bde R.F.A.

Army Form C. 2118

Place	Date	Hour	Summary of Events and Information	Remarks and references to Appendices
COLOGNE	1-9-19		Headquarters at DEUTZ. "A" "B" and "D" Batty's at POLL. "C" Batty at OVERATH.	
	2-9-19		Ordinary routine and training carried out.	
DEUTZ	3-9-19		do. do.	
	4-9-19		do do	
GERMANY	5-9-19		do do	
	6-9-19		Inspection carried out. Half holiday in afternoon	
	7-9-19		Church Parades for all denominations in morning. Half holiday in afternoon	
	8-9-19		Ordinary routine and training carried out	
	9-9-19		74 O.R.'s to 101 Concentration Camp LOZ6NE for dispersal All Ranks. Men	
	10-9-19		Ordinary routine afternoon	
	11-9-19		do	
	12-9-19		Ct Carter V.E.S. 19 S and 2 T mules to	
	13-9-19		Inspection carried out	

Army Form C. 2118.

Appx. 2.   WAR DIARY   190 Bde
            INTELLIGENCE SUMMARY.   R.F.A.
            (Erase heading not required.)

Place	Date	Hour	Summary of Events and Information	Remarks and references to Appendices
COLOGNE	14.9.19		Church parade for all denominations	
STUTZ	15.9.19		Games and training	
	16.9.19		Holiday given to the troops of the Division on account of the Pure Bone Show at OVERATH	
	17.9.19		Games, return and training	
	18.9.19		15 O.R's inspected to 1st Concentration Camp Cologne	
	19.9.19		Ordinary stable and training	
	20.9.19		do Infantry runners inspection	
	21.9.19		Church Parade for all denominations	
	22.9.19		14 O.R's inspected to Concentration Camp Cologne	
	23.9.19		8 O.R's do do	
	24.9.19		Capt & Adjt J H NEEDHAM & army spend leave to UK	
			Major C.E.G. WOOLCOMBE-ADAMS 3 weeks spend leave UK	
	25.9.19		25 O.R's to 1st Concentration Camp COLOGNE	
	26.9.19		All leave suspended under further orders. Infantry routine & training carried on as far as possible	

WAR DIARY Sheet 3. of 190th Bde R.F.A. Army Form C. 2118.
INTELLIGENCE SUMMARY.

(Erase heading not required.)

Place	Date	Hour	Summary of Events and Information	Remarks and references to Appendices
COLOGNE	27.9.19		Lt Col Captain F Penn MC D/190 to Army Animal Camp to review	
DEUTZ			Conducting Officer attended ceremony	
Germany			all movement of troops to the UK stopped	
	28.9.19		American Army Horse Show. Battery took 1st prize in jump and Tenn and hit goose in mess cart	
	29.9.19		32 "S" horses and mules to Divl. Reception Camp for sale	
	30.9.19		Getting ready for training. 6th Corps Horse Show	

D Barton
Lt Col
Comdg 190 Bde RFA

30/9/19

WAR DIARY

190th Bde RFA

INTELLIGENCE SUMMARY

(Erase heading not required.)

Army Form C. 2118.

Place	Date	Hour	Summary of Events and Information	Remarks and references to Appendices
Cocoanut	1.10.19		Major Seffrets 2i/c 4B Battery supple 2nd Lieut MILL	
Depot 2	2.10.19		Ordinary routine & training	
			Capt J H NEED HAM from leave delayed by strike	
Ismay	3.10.19		Ordinary routine & training GOC inspected AO's Batty	
	4.10.19		Mount Seffrets informed inspection taken Revd	
			Artillery Trials Symptoms on eyeheap	
	5.10.19		Church Parades. G.O.C. all denominations	
	6.10.19		Ordinary routine and training. E. Barker posted to	
				LDMAR per DuSEATI
	7.10.19		do	
	8.10.19		do	
	9.10.19		do	
	10.10.19		54 O.R.'s for our personal sent to Mil Convalescent Camp	
	11.10.19		40 O.R.'s for superior in Mil Convalescent Camp Cee GNE	
	11.10.19		Day holiday in honour of inspection during morning	
	12.10.19		Church Parade for all denominations 26 O.R.'s	
			departure to Mil Camp CeCGNE	
	13.10.19		25 O.R.'s for disposal Mil Camp CeCGNE	

Army Form C. 2118.

Sheet 2

WAR DIARY
INTELLIGENCE SUMMARY.
(Erase heading not required.)

Instructions regarding War Diaries and Intelligence Summaries are contained in F.S. Regs., Part II. and the Staff Manual respectively. Title pages will be prepared in manuscript.

Place	Date	Hour	Summary of Events and Information	Remarks and references to Appendices
COLOGNE	13/10/19		Brown assumed the 18 Bde RFA as acting OC Brigade for three farrow who has lived of this Bde	
SRITZ				
Janney out	14/10/19		(190 Bde RFA transferred to 157 Bde RFA 25 OR's to M1 Camp COLOGNE for disposal	
	15/10/19		23 do	
	16.10.19		18 do	
	17.10.19		20	
	18.10.19		15	
	19-10-19		Artillery stores repayment. Exchanged surveys with 18 Bde RFA.	
	20-10-19			
	21.10.19		Remounts: men cont[inue] for Jul 5 to 18 Bde RFA	
	22.10.19		fine marques and ammunition all handed over to Equipment Camp MERHEIM, meanwhile stores handed into ESD VI ICS LINDENTHAL. VI Corps	
			do	
			do	
	23.10.19		do	
	24.10.19			
			6 OR's Chungyn dispersed to UK	

WAR DIARY
INTELLIGENCE SUMMARY

Army Form C. 2118.

Sheet 3

Place	Date	Hour	Summary of Events and Information	Remarks and references to Appendices
COLOGNE	25.10.19	—	2 ORs to Mil Comt Cologne and 4 ORs to the OK BERRAY to	
DEUTZ	—	—	LANNER Lt DROMAD and Lt ALLISON	
January	—	—	11 Regular RA Officers posted to 182 Bde R.F.A for duty, there being no guns from which to report.	
	26.10.19	—	Nothing to report.	
	27.10.19	—	2nd Junior (major) Lt BARTER Lt DIRTH & 2Lt FALOTTON to Mil camp for appeal, also SOR Lt SHEPERD to Concentration Camp for dispersal (Lt DUMLEY Lt SHEERAN Gazed Lt DAWSON)	
	29.10.19	—	Captain J.M. NEEDHAM to 182 Bde R.F.A for duty, all recent regiments transferred to 182 Bde R.F.A for completion. Transfers to training Reserve Army have not continued	

Wm Carter
Capt.
OC 190 Bde RFA

19.10.19

www.ingramcontent.com/pod-product-compliance
Lightning Source LLC
Chambersburg PA
CBHW081524160426
43191CB00011B/1681